Development and its Discontents

Development and its Discontents

ANDY SUMNER

OXFORD
UNIVERSITY PRESS

OXFORD
UNIVERSITY PRESS

Great Clarendon Street, Oxford, OX2 6DP,
United Kingdom

Oxford University Press is a department of the University of Oxford.
It furthers the University's objective of excellence in research, scholarship,
and education by publishing worldwide. Oxford is a registered trade mark of
Oxford University Press in the UK and in certain other countries

Published in the United States of America by Oxford University Press
546 Fifth Avenue, New York, NY 10036, United States of America

British Library Cataloguing in Publication Data
Data available

Library of Congress Control Number: 2026934375

ISBN 9780198902874

DOI: 10.1093/9780198902904.001.0001

Printed and bound by
CPI Group (UK) Ltd., Croydon, CR0 4YY

The manufacturer's authorized representative in the EU for product safety is
Oxford University Press España S.A. of Parque Empresarial San Fernando de Henares,
Avenida de Castilla, 2 – 28830 Madrid (www.oup.es/en or product.safety@oup.com).
OUP España S.A. also acts as importer into Spain of products made by the manufacturer.

MIX
Paper | Supporting
responsible forestry
FSC www.fsc.org
FSC® C013604

Acknowledgements

The author would like to thank the following people for discussions related to the content of this book in some form or another going back several years: Imaduddin Abdullah, Saran Banluphanthunat, Pritish Behuria, Azral Bin Mazlan, Karina Batthyány, Pritish Behuria, Jelke Boesten, Basile Boulay, Ryan Briggs, Laura Camfield, Gilles Carbonnier, James Copestake, Andrea Cornwall, Salome Ecker, Andrew Fischer, Jorge Garcia-Arias, Marcin Grabowski, Brendan Howe, Rory Horner, David Hulme, Bhanubhatra Jittiang, Ravi Kanbur, Ray Kiely, Kyunghoon Kim, Ingrid Kvangraven, David Lewis, Simon Maxwell, Kate Meagher, Anisa Muzaffar, Nita Mishra, Iliana Olivié, Eduardo Ortiz-Juarez, Hugo Pinchon, Sebeka Plaatjie, Alfredo Saad-Filho, Diego Sanchez-Ancochea, María Santillán O'Shea, Ben Selwyn, Antonio Sianes Castaño, Paul Shaffer, Ashra Shrestha, Mayssoun Sukarieh, Raphael Susewind, Thomas Tanner, Susanne von Itter, Geof Wood, Michael Woolcock, and Arief Anshory Yusuf.

Contents

1
Introduction

Development and its Discontents. Andy Sumner, Oxford University Press. © Andy Sumner (2026).
DOI: 10.1093/9780198902904.003.0001

1.1 Introduction

The international order within which development takes places is in a state of flux. The post–Cold War order looks frayed. Geopolitical rivalry, weaker multilateralism, and widening global inequalities now shape how development is defined and debated. At the same time, policy challenges such as sustaining rising incomes, adapting to climate change, and addressing disparities are becoming more complex. These challenges highlight the importance of studying development especially so in the contemporary context. They also raise questions about what kind of theories or frameworks are required to understand development in such a turbulent world.

In this context, Development Studies, as a field of inquiry, is well-placed. It has long engaged with questions of global inequality, the legacies of imperialism, and contested visions of progress in and outside the 'Global South'.[1] Indeed, Development Studies stands as a well-established field of scholarly inquiry. It can demonstrate good health in terms of the longevity of scholarly journals, departments and institutes, associations, and teaching programmes. There are though intellectual tensions within Development Studies itself. There are diverse ways of thinking across Development Studies. These 'modes of thought' generate different positions on three continua: the framing of development (what development is), the scope of development (which countries are developing), and the onto-epistemology of development (how development can be known).[2]

The term modes of thought, used here and throughout this book, is related to Dow's (1990; 2002; 2007) discussion of the same idea within economics. It refers to the ways in which intellectual traditions shape reasoning and analysis. In the present context, it describes how contrasting modes of

[1] Throughout this book, the term 'Global South' is used to refer to low- and middle-income countries. It is used in this book as in recent years it has become the most common label for the group of countries that were previously defined as 'developing' and most of which were colonised. The term 'Global South' is however not without contention. Haug et al. (2021) refer to the term as a meta-category in world politics, meaning a classificatory lens rather than a fixed empirical region. They argue that while usage of 'Global South' has surged in recent scholarship, the category remains under-defined: the authors identify three dominant framings of socio-economic marginality, multilateral alliance/resistance, and positionality vis-à-vis hegemonic powers. Haug (2021) goes further and employs Edward Soja's 'Thirdspace' which is understood as a trialectic of material (Firstspace), imagined (Secondspace), and lived (Thirdspace) spatialities to interrogate how the term 'Global South' operates in both discourse and practice. They argue too that meanings vary materially (via development indicators), imaginatively (in geopolitical alliances), and experientially (in bureaucrats' everyday practices). Relatedly, see discussion of Sud and Sánchez-Ancochea (2022) who discuss the use of 'the South' as a concept.

[2] The combining of ontology and epistemology into 'onto-epistemological' is simply to highlight the interconnectedness of ontology and epistemology.

thought condition how development is conceptualised, what research questions are formulated, and which analytical approaches are favoured. Dow uses the concept to explore how economists structure knowledge within differing methodological traditions. A mode of thought is a shared set of assumptions and reasoning that guides inquiry. It brings together ontological views about the nature of reality, epistemological positions on what can be known, and methodological preferences concerning how investigation should be carried out. These shared commitments influence what is regarded as a legitimate question or method within a school of thought. In Dow's view, mainstream economics, particularly the neo-classical tradition, operates largely within a closed-system orientation that presumes stable relations and universal laws amenable to formal modelling.[3]

In Development Studies, as in Economics, each mode of thought shapes how knowledge about development is constructed. It also shapes explanation of phenomena and claims to know about development through its influence on reasoning and analysis. In Development Studies, these modes can be mapped along three continua. They are the framing of development, the scope of development, and the onto-epistemology of development. Continua are used as these are continuous characteristics that change across a spectrum. These continua build on, and thus extend, the typology presented in Sumner (2022; 2024) with a further dimension.[4] Different schools of thought within Development Studies can be loosely plotted on each continuum. The exact positioning will always be contentious and open to debate.

The book's contribution is to map these modes of thought. It is useful to explain why such mapping is helpful. First, the book contributes a contemporary extension to books that introduce Development Studies (e.g., Currie-Alder et al., 2014; Desai and Potter, 2014; Pattanaik, 2016; Peet and Hartwick, 2015; Sumner and Tribe, 2008; Willis, 2005). Second, the book updates the literature on the 'impasse' in Development Studies. This is timely given the internal differentiation visible in the field. The 1980s and 1990s impasse in Development Studies refers to a critical moment of theoretical and empirical

[3] See also Lawson (1997; 2003; 2019).

[4] In earlier iterations (e.g., Sumner, 2024), two of the continua were combined in a 2×2 approach which generated combinations between the 'framing' and 'scope' tensions. If there are two axes of (i) the framing of development as a systems transformation (i.e., the structural transformation of economic production) versus development as 'systems maintenance' or 'fixing' (i.e., triggering economic growth) and (ii) the scope of development as GS-centric in the first instance or universalist focus (meaning all countries), this results in a set of modes of thought. In abstract (and here not associated with a specific school of thought), this will generate the following implied 'ideal types' as follows: (i) systems transformation and GS-centric DS; (ii) systems maintenance/fixing and GS-centric DS; (iii) systems transformation and universalist DS; (iv) systems maintenance/fixing and universalistic DS.

disillusionment. It was marked by a deep questioning of core assumptions, methods, and normative orientations (see Booth, 1985; Munck and O'Hearn, 1999; Schuurman, 1993). It also included post-structuralist critique (e.g., Escobar, 1992; 1995). The book argues that a comparable 'new impasse' could emerge. The driver is a divergence of worldviews and critiques from within and outside Development Studies. The focus here is on the intellectual tensions. The objective is not to generate a false or meaningless consensus. It is to support greater interdisciplinarity within Development Studies. The route is better understanding of the differing modes of thought in the field.

The purpose of this introductory chapter is to orientate the reader. The chapter is structured as follows. Section 2 presents the competing origin stories of Development Studies. Section 3 turns the question of what binds, i.e., the commonalities across, Development Studies as a field of enquiry and raises the question of a new impasse. Section 4 then introduces the book structure. A summary of each chapter is also presented. Section 5 concludes.

1.2 Origin Stories of Development and Its Study

When, where, or how development and its study began remains a matter of considerable contestation.[5] One could trace the history to the social science disciplines on which Development Studies is largely based, which emerged as distinct in the late nineteenth century and early twentieth century (although the origins of social science can be traced further back). However, these are only constituent parts. The history of Development Studies as cross-disciplinary is most often associated with one of several origin stories. And, underlying these stories is a dialectic of imperialism and anti-imperialism intertwined.

Behuria and Sumner (2025) note a set of specific origin stories. One dates Development Studies to the colonial era. A second links it to classical development economics that emerged in the 1930s and 1940s, with prominence in the 1950s and 1960s. Much of this came from scholars involved in independence struggles and early post-independence planning. A third points to the Truman Doctrine and the 1949 speech to develop the 'underdeveloped areas'. A fourth links it to struggles for independence that led to formal decolonisation and anti-imperialist sentiment, consolidated at the Bandung

[5] This section draws substantially from Behuria and Sumner (2025). Thank you to Andrew Fischer for comments on the history of Development Studies.

Asia-Africa Conference. One could add within this both Soviet and Maoist influences. Soviet wartime planning and victory over Hitler inspired many southern development thinkers. In fact, (i) and (iii) can be merged into a story of Northern-led Development/Development Studies. In turn, (ii) and (iv) can be merged into a story of Southern-led Development or Development Studies. This also links to the emancipatory, anti-colonial struggle.

These competing narratives illustrate a dialectic between imperialism and resistance. They are in opposition but have co-evolved through mutual interaction. This has produced new forms of power and contestation that persist today and remain under the lens of Development Studies. The colonial genealogy connects Development Studies to its 'colonial roots' (Kothari, 2005b). Many Development Studies institutes were formed as a product of colonial history and numerous studies were made in, for example, British colonies in the late 1940s and 1950s (e.g., Gulliver, 1957; Lewis, 1953; Mayer, 1951; Peacock and Dosser, 1958). The neo-colonial Truman genealogy story links the rise of 'international development' and foreign aid to US Cold War objectives via Truman's 1949 'Point Four' programme for foreign policy. Helleiner (2014a; 2014b) challenges this narrative by showing that development ideas and institutional mandates emerged earlier and with significant non-Western influence. In keeping with this we discuss further.

A common reference point for the neo-colonial origin story is Truman's inaugural speech of 20 January 1949. It followed his re-election. The focus of the speech was US foreign policy in competition with the USSR. The USSR had incorporated Eastern Europe after WWII. The US was anxious about the spread of communist influence to other parts of the world. Not long before, the International Monetary Fund and the World Bank had been constituted. Both were established in 1944. The Marshall Plan to rebuild Europe began in 1948. Prosperity was framed as increasing production through technology. The focus was on countries already independent, such as Latin America, or soon-to-be independent countries in Asia and Africa. Truman's call was thus:

> ... we must embark on a bold new program for making the benefits of our scientific advances and industrial progress available for the improvement and growth of the underdeveloped areas. More than half the people of the world are living in conditions approaching misery ... our imponderable resources in technical knowledge are constantly growing and are inexhaustible.

In this lens, the genealogy of development and Development Studies can be traced to a longer intellectual history. It also links to the period of colonialism.

Accordingly, this perspective typically argues that Development Studies tends to pay too little attention to colonial history, which is a broader point worth reflecting on in Development Studies, regardless of mode or school of thought. For example, Kothari (2005b, pp. 47–48) stresses that Development Studies 'rarely acknowledges [its] colonial roots'. Roots in this context would be knowledge generated in or by the GN during and since colonialism about the Global South. Taking the Truman-origin story, modern Development Studies is simply built on colonial and extractive world view.

There is another origin story of Development Studies. It dates the field to classical development economics rather than neo-classical economics. That distinction matters here. The field of Development Studies later grew out of classical development economics in varied directions. Classical development economics was emerging in the 1930s. The English translation of Joseph Schumpeter (1911 [1934]) was published and Paul Rosenstein-Rodan's (1943, 1944) work was written during World War II and, like many early development economists, published in existing economic journals. Raúl Prebisch presented his manifesto on Latin American economic development at the Economic Commission for Latin America and the Caribbean (CEPAL)'s second conference in Havana in 1949 (see Prebisch, 1950 [1949]). Together, with Singer (1950), this laid the foundation for what became known as the Prebisch–Singer hypothesis, which argued that the terms of trade tend to decline over time for primary commodity exporters relative to manufacturers.[6] At around the same time, W. Arthur Lewis (1944; 1949; 1950; 1953) published studies on economic development in Jamaica, Puerto Rico, the British West Indies, and the Gold Coast. He followed these with the seminal dual economy model of economic development (Lewis, 1954). It is important to reiterate that the Economics (E) and Development Economics (DE) referred to here is classical E/DE in the sense of Lewis or Prebisch. It is not neo-classical E/DE. The differentiation matters because classical E/DE is interdisciplinary by definition. It treats the Global South as having different characteristics to the Global North in various ways. Hence, economic theory is not universal. However, neo-classical E/DE is not necessarily interdisciplinary by definition. It typically treats economic theory as universal. The latter is not interdisciplinary and is 'mono-economics'. The term refers to the claim that theories from

[6] Where Prebisch (1950) and Singer (1950) highlighted the structural disadvantages faced by primary-exporting economies in the international trading system and argued for industrialisation and state intervention to correct deteriorating terms of trade. This sat in contrast to Rostow (1960) who presented a linear, universalist model of national development based on stages of economic growth. In his framework, all countries could progress from 'traditional society' to 'maturity' and 'high mass consumption' through domestic savings, investment, and policy choices, largely independent of global structural constraints.

advanced economies cannot be transplanted straightforwardly to low- and middle-income countries (see Hirschman, 1981; see also Myrdal, 1957a). Neoclassical economics generally maintains that economic theory and principles are 'one size fits all'. It holds that they apply to all countries, rich and poor. In short, in its early incarnation, economics in Development Studies was classical E/DE. A foundational assumption was that the Global South is different to the Global North. These points matter because a recurring issue in Development Studies is the relationship with Economics. This includes both real and perceived aspects. Politics and sociology were evident in the early years of Development Studies. This pulled the field towards association with the interdisciplinarity of classical E/DE. That tradition took in aspects of politics and sociology.

Relatedly, there is an origin story of development and Development Studies linked to the 1955 Asia-Africa Conference in Bandung. The conference, which included many Global South leaders, intellectuals, and activists called for solidarity and unity among newly or soon-to-be independent nations, presented development in terms of 'catching up' and emancipation. These calls were made within the context of anti-imperialism, formal decolonisation, and the political ferment of the 1950s/1960s (Bernstein, 2005; Loxley, 2004). The Bandung conference itself was not the beginning of a Southern-oriented idea of development. Its antecedents were in earlier anti-colonial struggles. However, it was highly symbolic, and it was an important consolidating political event for the Non-Aligned Movement and anti-imperialism. Alongside the 1955 Bandung conference, other anti-imperialist movements influenced the study and practice of development. These included the black liberation movement in South Africa, the Soviet planning model, and Mao's 1949 triumph in China. Circling back to Bandung, India and Indonesia also led the Non-Aligned Movement. Within academic scholarship, anti-imperialist influences in Development Studies drew from the resurgence of Marxism, neo-Marxism, dependency theory, and Structuralism. They also drew from declarations of 'African Socialism' (see discussion of Fanon, 1961; and also, Nkrumah, 1965; Nyerere, 1966; 1968; Senghor, 1964).

The Bandung conference symbolised a GS-initiated anti-imperialist agenda.[7] The conference was organised by Indonesia, Burma, India, Ceylon, and Pakistan, with China also playing a key role. It brought together

[7] Relatedly, the Bandung conference was followed by a 1957 conference on African–Asian solidarity in Cairo and the 1961 Belgrade conference, where the Non-Aligned Movement was established. The latter conference laid the basis for the Group of 77 and hence a collective voice of the GS at the United Nations.

twenty-nine newly independent countries in Africa, Asia, and the Middle East, representing a large share of the world's population at that time, to discuss development in a post-colonial world, emphasising self-determination and equality. The context was many newly independent countries (and those soon-to-be independent) of the GS integrating into the global system as independent nations. The conference sought to promote African–Asian cooperation and to oppose colonialism and neo-colonialism in all its manifestations, implicitly expanding the critique to include the USSR as well as Western powers. It responded to a view put by Indian Prime Minister Nehru that was concerned about US foreign policy in Asia in particular and, in wider sense, about a lack of Western countries consulting with Asian nations on decisions affecting Asia. The Bandung conference's 'declaration on the promotion of world peace and cooperation' (also known as the 'Bandung Spirit' or 'Ten Principles') sits in juxtaposition to the Truman speech. The Bandung principles incorporated the principles of the UN charter and added five more on 'peaceful co-existence' from the China-India agreement of 1954; namely, respect for sovereignty, non-aggression, non-interference, equality, and peaceful co-existence. The declaration also pushed against the Truman speech by pointing to the need for the GS to break dependence on the industrialised countries by sharing their own technical assistance and expertise for development.

The anti-imperialism story of Development Studies, thus, emphasises political struggles for justice, independence, emancipation, and national development that many anti-colonial and post-independence leaders enunciated (see discussion in Bernstein, 2005; Harriss, 2005; Hulme and Toye, 2006; Wiegratz et al., 2023). This inspired Development Studies scholars, especially so in the 1950s/1960s. Much radical Development Studies was inspired by intellectuals from the Global South, particularly scholars in the United Nations Economic Commission for Latin America and the Caribbean (CEPAL, established in 1948), who contributed to Latin American Structuralist theory; critical voices at the United Nations Conference on Trade and Development (UNCTAD, established in 1964); and Latin American adaptions of neo-Marxian theory to the Global South (e.g., Cardoso and Faletto, 1979; dos Santos, 1970).

Dedicated research institutes and post-graduate programmes in Development Studies are often traced to the years after the 1950s and 1960s ferment. There were earlier programmes and institutes in the Global South that were establishing the field as early as the 1940s and 1950s. These included UNCEPAL, established in 1948, and the Economic Commission for Africa, established in 1958, among a set of UN regional commissions. There was also the National Council of Applied Economic Research in New Delhi, established in 1956. The Latin American Faculty of Social Sciences in Chile was established in 1957. Slightly later, the Institute of Statistical, Social and Economic Research at the University of Ghana was established in 1969. It evolved from the Economic Research Unit founded in 1962.

Around the same time, Development Studies courses emerged in the Global North. The University of Manchester had short courses in the 1950s. The International Institute of Social Studies in the Netherlands also had an early master's programme. Further back, the School of Oriental and African Studies was established in 1916. In the 1970s, the largest cross-country association of Development Studies was established. This was the European Association of Development Research and Training (EADI) at conferences in 1974 and 1975. Some national Development Studies associations were also created then. For example, the UK Development Studies Association was established in 1978 at Strathclyde, Glasgow. A set of conferences preceded it, beginning at the 'First National Development Research Conference' in 1971 at IDS Sussex. Further meetings took place in 1973 in East Anglia and in 1976 in Manchester (see for more detailed history, Tribe, 2009). Field-specific journals in Development Studies were launched in the 1960s and 1970s. Examples include the Journal of Development Studies, Development and Change, World Development, and Third World Quarterly. They began in 1964, 1970, 1973, and 1979, respectively. There are older journals such as Economic Development and Cultural Change established in 1952. There are also important journals established earlier and based in the Global South. Social and Economic Studies, published by the University of the West Indies, was established in 1953 and published translated work from Latin America. The CEPAL Review and CODESRIA's Africa Development were both founded in 1976.[8]

Development Studies in the mid-2020s is evident in both the Global North and the Global South. It appears in over 150 university post-graduate courses around the world according to the QS rankings (QS, 2025). This number has expanded over the decade since 2015, when such rankings began. A caveat is necessary. The QS-ranked list of post-graduate teaching in Development Studies is not necessarily comprehensive. Some programmes may not be listed, and in many cases, Development Studies programmes may lack visibility. The list, with its limitations, shows that post-graduate Development Studies programmes exist in a wide range of Global South countries as well as the Global North. Of at least thirty-eight countries with post-graduate Development

[8] Even relatively, 'new' journals, such as the European Journal of Development Research (established in 1989), have been in existence for over thirty-five years.

Table 1.1 Worldwide post-graduate programmes of Development Studies by regions ranked in the QS, 2025

	Number of countries with Development Studies programmes	Total number of universities with Development Studies programmes
Global South		
Africa	4	10
Asia excluding Japan	11	25
Latin America and the Caribbean	6	10
Global North		
USA and Canada	2	31
Europe	12	59
Australia and New Zealand	2	15
Japan	1	2
Total	38	152

Source: QS (2025).

Studies programmes, slightly less than half are in the Global North and slightly more than half are in the Global South. The latter is extended to include the 'historical Global South', including South Korea (see Table 1.1). There are far more universities with Development Studies programmes in the Global North. Of 152 universities globally, 107 are in the Global North. Europe has a particular concentration, with fifty-nine universities across twelve countries. This may reflect the interdisciplinarity found in European universities and the history of Europe and the Global South. The QS (2025) shows that there are globally ranked Development Studies post-graduate programmes in Asia, Africa, and Latin America. Examples include Argentina, Brazil, Chile, China, Colombia, Egypt, Ghana, India, Indonesia, Japan, Kenya, Malaysia, Mexico, Peru, South Africa, South Korea, Thailand, and Uganda. There are indications that Development Studies remains as much an area of study in the Global South as in the Global North. This holds at least in terms of numbers of countries with programmes, even if Europe has a concentration. It is not a surprise that there are multiple origin stories and multiple modes of thought in Development Studies.

As is evident, Development Studies has clear part of its history in Europe, with numerous departments and institutes of Development Studies based in (Western) European countries with a particular concentration in the UK (twenty-four of fifty-nine universities in Europe with post-graduate

Development Studies programmes) and the Netherlands (seven universities). Outside Europe, the US (twenty-seven universities), Australia (eleven), and South Africa (seven) are also notable.

Some attribute Development Studies' prominent presence in Europe to the continent's colonial history. There are also other factors. These include the establishment of interdisciplinary departments of Development Studies, which is more common in some European countries. This has supported the expansion of Development Studies intellectually and institutionally. Further, the inspiration for many scholars in Development Studies in the GN has been a sense of solidarity with the radical political struggles of anti-imperialism in the GS (Bernstein, 2005). Many who situate their research and teaching in Development Studies are discontent with elements of mainstream or orthodox development. Examples include the neo-colonial structure of the global economy, 'extractive' development, Northern aid-driven development, or the pursuit of a capitalist modernity aligned with Northern interests. A common thread is discontent with orthodox development, which motivates this book's title.

There are many Global North institutes and scholars. Development Studies was though, in its origins, as much a southern-led field as it was northern-led. It remains so to a considerable extent. A lot of the dynamic theorisation was generated from the south, especially the more critical theorising. In fact, the evolution of Development Studies has to some extent been characterised by the interaction between the GS-GN tension. Specifically, on one side, there exists scholarship centered on the Global South, driven by the challenges and aspirations of anti-imperialism and decolonisation. On the other hand, the major Northern powers, i.e., United States and Europe, and their foreign policy and aid agencies have endeavoured to influence the evolution of the field, at least in part to establish legitimacy in the post-colonial era and to support their interests. Many of these struggles continue today reflecting the diversity of the intellectual and institutional landscape of Development Studies.

Development Studies has then a history in both the Global South and the Global North. Tensions and struggles then and now remain similar. They include a Southern-oriented scholarship motivated by anti-imperialism and solidarity from Global North scholars, versus Northern political interests shaping the field. This linked to the need to support aid administrations. That has shifted with the decline in the number of countries where aid is important and the rise in countries where aid is less relevant due to domestic resources. There is also a shift of Northern interests back towards merging development and foreign policy. The question thus arises of what then binds Development Studies as a field of inquiry as well as questions of impasses old and new.

1.3 Commonalities, Cohesion, and the Impasse

Scholars such as Schuurman (1993), Martinussen (1997), and Munck and O'Hearn (1999) described the 1980s and 1990s impasse as a moment of reflection and critique. They saw a crisis or deadlock in which Development Studies had reached limits of explanatory and practical relevance due to theoretical, empirical, and analytical failings, and utility concerns (see Booth, 1985; Edwards, 1989). Post-structuralist critiques were also central (e.g., Escobar, 1992; 1995).

The 1980s and 1990s impasse was triggered by recognition that dominant development theories had failed to explain or resolve persistent under- or maldevelopment in developing countries. These included modernisation theory, dependency theory, and variants. The 'grand theories' were increasingly seen as too deterministic or teleological. Further, that the development project, particularly under the post-war modernisation paradigm and later under structural adjustment, was seen to have failed to deliver meaningful and sustained improvements in wellbeing. Disillusionment with top-down, state-led as well as market-led development approaches fed into this. The field faced a normative crisis: who defines development, and for whom? The universalist assumptions of development were increasingly critiqued for being Eurocentric, paternalistic, or depoliticising. Post-structuralist critiques argued that development was not just a set of policies or outcomes. It was a mode of power and knowledge that created subjects and spaces of intervention (e.g., Escobar, 1992; 1995). This challenged the legitimacy of development itself as a project.

The 1980s/90s impasse was also the beginning (or at least the visible beginning) of intellectual differentiation. Thus, the 'impasse' was not just about failure but also about a lack of coherence across increasingly diverse and often incompatible approaches, economic, political, cultural, postcolonial, and feminist, leading to debates about whether Development Studies could or should remain a coherent field.

The book in hand argues that there are the signs of a similar impasse emerging in contemporary intellectual tensions in the sense that critiques from within and outside Development Studies and the extent of diversity raise questions about the coherence of the field which are likely to continue. The book focuses on these set of contemporary tensions that underlie the ongoing internal differentiation of Development Studies and a nascent sense of a new impasse emerging in the field.

This new impasse is a polarisation between sometimes wildly differing modes of thought. The differences relate to the framing, scope, and onto-epistemology of development and its study. More worryingly, there are signs that some schools within Development Studies view other schools in Development Studies as oppressive or part of the problem. The basis of these critiques varies. These include methodological softness or lack of theoretical depth and colonial intent. One strong illustration of this is Rutazibwa's (2019, p. 162) call to eliminate Development Studies completely, which is defined as having a close association with aid (even to be synonymous). Specifically, it is argued that 'we need to find ways to go beyond critiquing and deconstructing [Development Studies], and seriously considering getting rid of it ... we need to fight the desire to hold on to Development Studies' (Rutazibwa, 2018, p. 162). Development Studies is further accused of perpetuating global inequality through racial hierarchies, subjectification of the 'Other', and the geopolitics of knowledge production. The latter refers to knowledge produced in and by scholars and research-funding agencies in the North about the countries and people of the Global South. Some decolonial scholars go further and argue that southern scholars and policy elites who are trained in Northern modes of thinking are part of the reproduction of coloniality.

Calls to 'decolonise' knowledge are evident not only in Development Studies but across the social sciences and beyond and have grown louder over the last decade. Hull (2021) offers a useful differentiation of two often conflated concepts, of 'intellectual decolonisation' and of 'decoloniality' (See also, Hull, 2019; 2022). The former, which is evident to some degree across all of Development Studies, aims at 'pluralising' knowledge beyond North American/European-dominated scholarship. To some, this simply implies drawing from scholarship around the world, or privileging theories and ideas from GS scholars. To others, it is 'intellectual decolonisation' or a stronger shift of teaching and research towards a place where the Northern and/or White voice/'gaze' (Pailey, 2020) is not privileged, where stronger institutional positions address racial hierarchies across teaching and research, and/or where equitable international collaborations are pursued. In contrast, the latter, decolonial theory, is a specific body of theory that argues that Western knowledge about the Global South is innately racist and Eurocentric, as it is to justify the imposition of capitalist modernity on the Global South during and since colonisation. And it is blind to questions of race and racism. Patel (2020) for illustration presents a review of articles in major Development

Studies journals and finds that only thirty-two of over 9,000 papers surveyed mention the words 'race', 'racial', or 'racism'.[9] Post-Structuralists have argued that many things could be counted as knowledge, not only what is published in scientific journals, and that there is no hierarchy of 'scientific' knowledge over 'non-scientific' knowledge. The discussion on these matters has triggered some sense of an existential crisis, for some but not all, in Development Studies and a growing number of Development Studies programmes are grappling with these questions.

The underpinnings of the potential new impasse are also about major world changes, such as the current flux in the international order, and the ability of not only of Development Studies to understand and explain such changes. There is the decolonisation critique from within Development Studies; that Development Studies is part of the problem; but also, the bifurcation of the Global South between relatively small set of countries that have got barely better off in living standards since the 1970s and are highly aid dependent, and the majority of countries in the GS that are 'post-ODA', meaning aid no longer matters, though even post-ODA GS countries remain in a subordinate position in the global political economy. In other words, the GS has bifurcated between a set of 'stuck', very poor, and Official Development Assistance (ODA)-dependent countries, where living standards have not improved substantially and a set of dynamic, middle-income countries that have experienced sustained rising average incomes and are, as a consequence, post-ODA countries. Relatedly, there is the issue of Development Studies seeking to understand and explain development in a dramatically changing context evident in for example, the emergence of a multi-polar world, a new era of geopoliticisation of development and a stronger sense of collective agency in the 'New South' (see Ishmael, 2024), alongside the continuing and accelerating existential threat climate change poses, especially so in the Global South. In short, a new impasse, if it fully emerges, will be grappling with a range of issues similar to the last impasse, namely the ability to explain development amid rapid global change.

In this context, this book's objective is to foster reflection on the complexities inherent in the field of study and to stimulate further scholarly debate by highlighting differences in knowledge foundations and worldviews within

[9] Further, Patel (2020) notes only twenty-four of these thirty-two engage with race in its own right or in knowledge production and validation. In the other eight studies, race is either a variable in quantitative studies and sits within development economics rather than Development Studies or it is a descriptive container (p. 1471). Only seven papers explore race as a construct that 'does something' and is socially situated in, for example, the politics of race, racial hierarchy, or racial difference.

Development Studies and of course, the author's perspective is partial and shaped by where the author sits in the world as well as their biases. The book argues that fragmentation will continue as the divides become more entrenched. The risk is that Development Studies becomes a set of echo chambers evolving in quite different directions and as a result, the cohesiveness of Development Studies is questioned. To use an analogy: imagine there are centripetal forces and centrifugal forces in any area of knowledge enquiry. The centripetal forces pull the area of enquiry together in for example similar worldviews and common ways of approaching enquiry or similar modes of thought. In contrast, the centrifugal forces push the area of enquiry apart in differing worldviews and uncommon ways of approaching enquiry or different modes of thought. When the forces pulling outwards and apart become stronger than the forces pulling inward, objects may fly off altogether.

This all sounds rather dramatic. Is it overkill? Perhaps. A lack of consensus is inherent in all fields of inquiry. However, in Development Studies, the differences concern some fundamental questions about the modes of thought (the framing, scope, and onto-epistemology of development) and thus the worldview and approaches to the study of development. One could note that ignoring the differences or sweeping them under the carpet is one strategy for harmony though it risks marginalising some modes of thought as a result of the dominance of other modes of thought. This book seeks to do the opposite. It seeks to bring the different modes of thought to the fore even if that leads to discomfort and as Abbott (2002, p. 210) notes eloquently, '[e]very academic knows the experience of reading something from outside his or her discipline and knows the unsettling feeling it induces'.

What then binds Development Studies as a field of inquiry? In the search for self-identity, commonalities have emerged across Development Studies though each with inherent tensions themselves (see discussion in Baud et al., 2019; Molteberg and Bergstrøm, 2000; Bergstrøm and Molteberg, 2000; Harriss, 2002; Hulme and Toye, 2006; Kothari et al., 2005b; Melber et al., 2024; Molteberg and Bergstrøm 2000). First, Development Studies investigates 'development', meaning the need for 'good change' of some kind (in the words of Chambers, 2004; 2012). More simply, the change that happens through this may be both 'willed' or orchestrated change (i.e., state planning) or unintentional, day-to-day life, or the dialectic between both to draw from Cowen and Shenton (1996) and Hart (2001; 2002; 2010). The definition of what constitutes good or bad 'change' or development, and for whom, remains highly contested (as do the conditions or mechanisms under any form of development is possible). This is the basis of the 'framing' tension (see Chapter 3) in the sense of should development be of a radical transformatory nature or reform and fixing of systems. Further, development can mean change (e.g., urbanisation), but it can also mean studying non-change or stagnation (e.g., persistent poverty). And although Development Studies is cross-disciplinary, some disciplines mix more easily than others, and some disciplines are hard to mix. Further, true inter- or even trans-disciplinarity is difficult and fraught with its own complexities.

Second, Development Studies has generally been concerned with development in the Global South, most of which was colonised by (now) 'developed' countries or the 'North'. Developed countries themselves are ambiguously situated in the study of development in the Global South. Sometimes, they are included explicitly or implicitly; in other instances, developed countries are absent altogether. This is the basis of the 'scope' tension (see Chapter 4). It can be added that Development Studies tend to be applied, instrumental, or normative in orientation in the sense that knowledge is not generated for its own sake, as one finds in other areas of scholarly inquiry, but rather to understand real-world problems (even when theorising). Briggs (2024) provides empirical evidence of this in that he concludes that the majority of Development Studies academics do subscribe to what can be labelled 'beneficentrism', which is a philosophical position that prioritises worldwide wellbeing (See Chappell, 2024).[10] This normative agenda raises questions of onto-epistemology in terms of what social reality is (ontology) and what can be known (epistemology) and in particular what the relationship between the researcher and the researched is, not only in terms of objectivity/subjectivity and positivism/constructivism but also who decides what to research and how, as well as who does the research and who benefits (see Chapter 5).

In short, although debates on the self-identity of Development Studies continue, there is some common understanding on Development Studies being about 'development' and having a normative or real-world and cross-disciplinary orientation. It has been generally focused on the Global South though this is now being questioned and how GN is or is not incorporated in the study remains contentious. That said, there is no single Development Studies. Instead, as alluded to before, there are competing modes of thought that hold contrasting normative, ontological, and theoretical assumptions.

[10] Briggs (2024) surveyed scholars of Development Studies and noted that students and faculty members generally express confidence in Development Studies' capacity to effect positive change. However, it is noteworthy that this optimism tends to diminish as students progress through their programme of study.

Those modes of thought become more visible when schools of thought are discussed directly (see Chapter 2).

What are those multiple and competing ways of knowing about development? This book contends that while there exists a shared understanding that Development Studies revolves around the (highly contested) concept of 'development' and adopts a cross-disciplinary (an umbrella term for all mixing of disciplines, not just interdisciplinarity), as well as normative or real-world orientation (the discontent noted), the field is not a monolithic entity. Rather, it comprises a range of competing ways of knowing characterised by contrasting modes of thought, delineated along a set of fault lines. In other words, there is a set of fundamental differences within Development Studies on what is to be studied, where, and how.

So, are the same drivers that triggered the 1980s/1990s impasse in Development Studies still present today? This book argues that they are though with some shifts. More than thirty years on, it is pertinent to ask whether the conditions that triggered that impasse persist, have been resolved, or have taken new forms. The impasse was less a historical episode and more the beginning of an ongoing process of epistemological and normative questioning. The field has, in many ways, institutionalised critique, but this has not necessarily translated into more coherence and intellectual transformation. Rather than viewing the impasse as a crisis overcome, it may be more appropriate to understand Development Studies today as characterised by a condition of productive instability, in which critical reflection is both necessary and permanent. While some features have evolved or been mitigated, others appear more entrenched or intensified. In particular, the diverging theoretical frameworks, the persistence of unequal development outcomes, and the slow pace of epistemic and institutional reform suggest that the field now operates in that condition of productivity instability, rather than post-impasse resolution. No single school is hegemonic or doing 'normal science' in the Kuhnian sense.

Many features of the 1980s–1990s impasse persist today, in altered form. For example, the original impasse was shaped by widespread dissatisfaction with grand theoretical frameworks which had failed to provide convincing or predictive accounts of development processes. In response, Development Studies has embraced a broader spectrum of theoretical perspectives. This pluralisation has enriched the field but has also deepened its internal differentiation. There is little consensus on what constitutes 'development' or a 'good society', raising questions about the loss of a shared conceptual core.

The 1980s and 1990s were also marked by a loss of confidence in both state-led and market-driven development strategies, particularly in the wake of structural adjustment. Today, although global extreme monetary poverty has declined, due to growth in China, many empirical challenges remain acute. Inequality, precarious livelihoods, and environmental degradation have become more prominent. The COVID-19 pandemic, climate crisis, and renewed debt burdens in many GS countries have amplified scepticism regarding the ability of prevailing development models to produce positive outcomes. The scale and urgency of contemporary challenges arguably exceed those faced in the earlier period, notably the existential challenge of climate change.

The original impasse also catalysed a critical interrogation of the Eurocentric and universalist assumptions underpinning the study of development. Contemporary Development Studies has taken up these points and anti-imperialism, decolonisation, epistemic justice, and the politics of positionality have become evident. Nonetheless, institutional and funding architectures remain largely unchanged. Power asymmetries between global North and South, and within the South, continue to shape who defines development, who benefits, and 'whose reality counts' to use Chamber's (1997) book title.

The impasse of the 1980s/1990s also raised fundamental questions about the identity of Development Studies, as a field of enquiry. These questions remain unresolved. Development Studies continues to operate across disciplinary boundaries, drawing from economics, anthropology, political science, sociology, and geography. This cross-disciplinarity is a strength, but it also exacerbates tensions about coherence and direction. And the field's conceptual boundaries remain fluid and contested. Although the field has responded constructively to the original impasse through openness to new theories, and an increased willingness to challenge established power structures, many of the epistemic, normative, and structural tensions that defined the impasse remain unresolved or have re-emerged in more complex forms. If the original impasse signalled a moment of crisis, it might be more accurate to say DS is now framed by a continual questioning of its own assumptions, boundaries, and purpose. In short, a perpetual crisis of self-identity and reinvention and it is this which the book in hand seeks to speak to.

1.4 This Book and Its Structure

This book is structured as follows: Following this introductory chapter, Chapter 2 provides in more detail discussion on the different modes of thought and their concrete exemplars in schools of thought in Development Studies.

Initially, the chapter discusses shifts in the social science since the visible emergence of Development Studies to understand the influences on Development Studies before turning to differentiation within Development Studies. The chapter argues that the emergence of Development Studies within social science has been influenced to a considerable extent by major but contradictory transformations, leading to splits in the social sciences. First, the significant shift away from positivism. At the same time, the imperialism of neo-classical economics, i.e., positivistic, thinking that has become more evident across the social sciences.[11] Over time, these currents have contributed to greater fragmentation in Development Studies it is argued.

Chapters 3, 4, and 5 then turn to the framing, scope, and onto-epistemology of development. In Chapter 3, the discussion is about whether development should be framed as a system transformation in some sense, either materially or non-materially (with material consequences, i.e., changing what is valued) or systems fixing. The former describes a transformation from traditional societies to modernity and tends to be an economic transition. The latter perspective counters this material transition and instead calls for the transformation of subjectivities or of what is valued, moving away from prioritising modernity and economic assets. The chapter argues that first, development can be conceptualised as a material process and/or outcome versus a discourse with intentional/willed aspects. That said, following Hart and Cowen-Shenton, these are not separate to unintentional/unwilled aspects (day-to-day life or ground-level politics), as they have often been misinterpreted. In fact, as the authors intended, there is an interplay or dialectic. Further, it is argued that there is a need to reclaim the idea of 'Big–D' or 'willed' development, which is often viewed as normatively problematic and top-down, aid-industry-driven. However, in a world where much of the GS is 'post-ODA', and ODA is no longer significant vis-à-vis domestic resources, and in line with the emancipatory declarations of independence and the Bandung conference, Big–D or willed development could, in principle, be an emancipatory and GS-centred framing. Second, the chapter argues that development should be transformatory in nature, with an emphasis on socio-economic transformation, because a modest amount of good change or systems fixing does not suffice to alter people's life chances or a country's prospects. Further, given the implied energy needs and resource extraction, it is for the GN to change its per capita energy use to accommodate the GS aspirations for socio-economic transformation

[11] For many, Development Studies defined itself then and now in opposition to the orthodox neo-classical economic approach, and in favour of some form of heterodoxy.

or at least to leave the door open to the GS as an option and not 'kicking away the ladder' in the words of Chang (2002). Modest reduction in extreme poverty and illbeing, is insufficient and has left aid-dependent GS countries still with much poverty and a partial and stalling transformation and post-ODA GS countries remain in a subordinate place in the hierarchy of the global economy with large pockets of absolute poverty and precarity despite economic growth. Indeed, most ODA-dependent GS countries have barely started the pathway to transformation, while most post-ODA countries face a stalled national economic transformation or even regression. The chapter discusses these empirical points.

Chapter 4 focuses on the scope of development and which countries DS is to study. Specifically, does Seers' (1963) 'special case' argument still stand sixty years later? In other words, are countries in the GN and GS still fundamentally different in terms of national socio-economic characteristics as well as their position in the world? The chapter argues that first, the GS and even post-ODA GS countries retain many of the structural characteristics identified by Seers making any discussion about mean income convergence questionable. Second, the chapter posits there are common sources of problems but different manifestations and ability to respond in the GS/GN, even in the post-aid GS. Third, the GN continues to hold power in the global economy and controls the prospects for development of the GS. Thus, this chapter argues to retain the GS/GN demarcation as a reflection of global hierarchy, albeit with an update taking note of the bifurcation within the GS and the need for greater emphasis on studying the hierarchy itself in the international political economy.

Chapter 5 focuses on the onto-epistemological of development. The chapter argues that the different framing and scope of development imply onto-epistemological consequences. These different ways of understanding and knowing the world need to be bought to the fore, given they present a crucial difference between scholars' understanding of development. For illustration, power is understood quite differently across Development Studies as epistemic or material in nature. It is argued that decolonisation is both epistemic and material, but reframed critical modernity should be supported for its liberating and emancipatory potential. In other words, Development Studies should pursue intellectual decolonisation but remain robust in its critique, too, on the material political economy dimensions of anti-imperialism. Furthermore, the concept of 'intellectual decolonisation' should be disentangled from decolonial theory. This is because the former is a different matter from the latter, with intellectual decolonisation being a concern across Development Studies and in fact all social sciences. Further, it is important not to lose sight of the interplay and trade-offs between conceptualising decolonisation primarily as either a material or epistemic concern. Finally, the book concludes with Chapter 6, which draws together the discussions of the book and looks to future scenarios for Development Studies.

1.5 Conclusion

This introductory chapter has sought to situate the argument and purpose of the book within the historical evolution of Development Studies. While the field remains institutionally vibrant and widely taught across both the Global North and Global South, it is also characterised by intellectual differentiation and unresolved tensions. These tensions concern not only the framing of development, the geographical and analytical scope of inquiry, and the onto-epistemological foundations of knowledge production, but also the divergent worldviews and normative positions that underpin them.

Development Studies, from its inception, has been shaped by competing genealogies, imperial and anti-imperial, technocratic and emancipatory, Northern-led and Southern-driven. These competing origin stories remain embedded in contemporary debates and continue to shape both the substance and the politics of the field. The dialectic of imperialism and resistance is not simply a legacy to be studied. It is a living tension that continues to animate intellectual and institutional struggles.

The author's view is that Development Studies is currently facing an inflection point, and potentially a new impasse, not necessarily of failure, as in the 1980s and 1990s, but one of dissonance and disjuncture. This impasse is not a singular crisis but a structural condition: a set of quite different modes of thought that risks the coherence and common purpose of the field. In this view, Development Studies is pulled between centripetal and centrifugal forces: while common concerns about development, inequality, and justice continue to bind many scholars, increasingly divergent ontological, epistemological, and normative perspectives threaten to pull the field apart into incommensurable enclaves.

Thus, at the heart of this book is a call not for consensus but for recognition of the diversity of modes of thought that exist within Development Studies. And of the ways in which these modes shape what is studied, how it is studied, and to what ends. Mapping these intellectual differences, however uncomfortable, is a necessary step towards more dialogue within the field and boundary crossing. If Development Studies is to remain a meaningful area of inquiry, it should not shy away from discussing internal tensions.

The chapters that follow take up these points. They examine in more detail the different modes of thought in Development Studies and the concrete schools of thought that give them form. They explore the implications of these modes for how development is framed (Chapter 3), where development is studied (Chapter 4), and how development is known (Chapter 5). Together, they offer a discussion on the intellectual heterogeneity of the field and the fault lines. The concluding chapter (Chapter 6) returns to the key themes introduced here and considers the possibilities for navigating Development Studies' productive instability in the years ahead.

2
The Study of Development

Development and its Discontents. Andy Sumner, Oxford University Press. © Andy Sumner (2026).
DOI: 10.1093/9780198902904.003.0002

2.1 Introduction

Chapter 1 outlined the rationale, structure, and contribution of this book. It also presented competing origin stories of Development Studies, highlighting the dialectic of imperialism and anti-imperialism that has shaped the field. This chapter now turns to the contemporary study of development itself. It considers the intellectual currents in the social sciences that have influenced Development Studies, the cross-disciplinary nature of the field, and the underlying 'knowledge foundations' that differentiate modes of thought within the field.

Development Studies, while situated within the social sciences, typically draws from or combines more than one of economics, sociology, anthropology, politics, and geography (Jackson, 2002; Kanbur, 2002). The chapter thus begins by examining broad shifts in the social sciences since WWII, given the influence of such shifts on the formation and evolution of Development Studies. The chapter then explores the question of cross-disciplinarity in Development Studies. Finally, the chapter discusses the field's knowledge foundations, drawing on Bevan's (2007) typology of 'building blocks' of knowledge, to explore how these vary across modes and schools of thought in Development Studies. This discussion lays the groundwork for Chapters 3, 4, and 5.

The core arguments of this chapter are as follows. First, the emergence and trajectory of Development Studies has been shaped by contradictory shifts in the wider social sciences. On the one hand, there has been a growing questioning of positivism. On the other, the increasing influence of neoclassical economics and its imperialist tendencies (Fine, 2002). Second, that Development Studies is better characterised as cross-disciplinary rather than disciplinary: it lacks the core concepts, methods, or theories that typically define a discipline. There is clear evidence of multidisciplinarity, and some evidence of interdisciplinarity. Deeper forms of interdisciplinarity are rarer, likely because it is more feasible to combine only a small number of disciplines, and some disciplines are more mixable than others. Third, the chapter presents the set of continua to map the modes of thought within Development Studies, which are then used to situate exemplar schools of thought and to discuss variation in knowledge foundations across Development Studies.

The chapter is structured as follows. Section 2 explores major shifts in the social sciences and their relevance for Development Studies. Section 3 considers the nature of cross-disciplinarity in Development Studies. Section 4 examines internal differentiation within Development Studies using Bevan's knowledge-building blocks. Section 5 concludes.

2.2 Currents in the Social Sciences and Their Influence on Development Studies

This section explores key intellectual currents in the social sciences since the mid-twentieth century and their influence on the emergence and evolution of Development Studies. These broader currents have significantly shaped the field of Development Studies, particularly by contributing to Development Studies' internal diversity.

Development Studies has always been shaped by social science disciplines and has been responsive to wider trends and tensions across them. Three particularly influential currents have been: First, the rise of critical political economy, often led by scholars from the Global South. Second, the proliferation of post-structuralist and constructivist thought. Third, the ascendancy of neo-classical economics and its spread to, amid resistance from, the social sciences, what Fine (2002) terms 'economic imperialism' and fourth, the rise of institutionalist thinking. These currents have shaped not only the conceptual and methodological tools employed in Development Studies, but also the ways in which development is framed, the scope of who and what constitutes the 'developing world', and the field's underlying onto-epistemological assumptions.

The first influential current stems from the emergence of critical political economy, especially as developed by Global South scholars responding to structural inequalities in the global political economy. This critique of orthodox economics was foundational to the development of dependency theory (Cardoso and Faletto, 1979), world-systems analysis (1974a; 1980; 1989; 2011), and broader traditions of structuralist thought, including Latin American structuralism and African political economy (Amin, 1976). These approaches reject universal 'mono-economics' and stress history, structural constraints, and the embedding of national trajectories in global capitalism.

In terms of the framing continuum, these approaches typically locate development as a question of systemic transformation rather than incremental change or technical fixes. In other words, Development Studies is framed as a response to historically structured inequality and dependency, often requiring structural shifts in global and national political economies. Regarding the scope continuum, critical political economy tends to differentiate strongly between the Global South and Global North, viewing the South as shaped by structurally subordinate positions in global capitalism. On the onto-epistemological continuum, these approaches tend to adopt realist or materialist ontologies and critical epistemologies, grounded in historical and structural analysis of social processes.

A second influential shift has been the emergence and spread of post-structuralist and constructivist thought across the social sciences. Rooted in the work of Foucault (1970; 1972; 1977; 1980; 1991), Said (1978; 1983; 1993), and Spivak (1988), and with some Bourdieu (1984; 1986; 1989; 1990) influences this current challenged foundational assumptions about objectivity, universality, and neutrality in social science. Said's (1978; see also 1983; 1993) *Orientalism* has been particularly influential in Development Studies. It argued that the Western scholarship, literature and institutions has historically constructed 'the Orient' or the East and by extension, the Global South through a discursive framework that positions non-Western people as exotic, irrational, and inferior and and thus in need of external intervention or management by the West. In a similar way, drawing on Foucault's (1991) concept of *governmentality*, post-structuralist critiques have highlighted the role of development discourse in constituting docile subjects and spaces for intervention (Escobar, 1995; Ferguson, 1990). These approaches emphasise the power-knowledge nexus in the construction of social realities.

Said's critique of *Orientalism* deserves further attention given its continuing resonance in Development Studies. He argued that Western cultural and intellectual traditions have historically framed the 'Orient' through a set of essentialised and binary oppositions, irrational versus rational, despotic versus democratic, backward versus modern, which legitimised colonial control and continue to inform development imaginaries. Said (1983; 1993) contended that all texts are 'worldly' meaning embedded in specific historical and political circumstances and the canonical literary and cultural texts of European imperialism were not merely reflections of empire but active participants in it. Orientalism is not only a literary tradition but a power-knowledge system that justifies intervention and subordination. Said's influence is foundational to post-development, postcolonial, and decolonial schools of thought in Development Studies. At the same time, Said's work has not gone uncontested. Amin (1989; 1997), for example, critiqued what he saw as the culturalism inherent in post-structuralist accounts. Amin argued that such approaches risk essentialising culture and neglecting historical materialism and structural political economy. He questioned whether culture, as portrayed in post-structuralist critique, is a stable and enduring driver of history. For Amin, Eurocentrism is not just discursive but also institutional and economic, a function of capitalism and imperialism, not merely representation. This debate between Said and Amin continues to shape tensions in Development Studies between discursive and materialist approaches, tensions that play out clearly across the three continua of framing, scope, and onto-epistemology.

In relation to the framing continuum, post-structuralist perspectives typically reject structural or material framings of development in favour of discursive and deconstructive approaches (i.e., systems transformation of what is valued). Development is not a neutral or technical process but a contested set of meanings and representations. On scope, post-structuralist work de-emphasises North–South binaries and examines how such categories are constructed and maintained. Onto-epistemologically, post-structuralist perspectives embrace social constructivism and relativism, rejecting positivist assumptions and foregrounding positionality, reflexivity, and the situated nature of knowledge production.

The third major current has been the increasing dominance of neo-classical economics and its expansion beyond its disciplinary boundaries, a trend Fine (2002) characterises as 'economic imperialism'. According to Fine, this expansion involves the diffusion of neo-classical assumptions, such as rational choice, market efficiency, and methodological individualism, into domains traditionally occupied by other social sciences. This trend has narrowed the conceptual space for alternative understandings of development, often crowding out normative concerns such as justice, redistribution, and historical context. Fine (2002) identifies three dimensions of economic imperialism. First is the hegemony of neo-classical framing of issues, which privileges market-based solutions and frames state intervention as legitimate only in cases of 'market failure'. Second is the colonisation of other disciplines, whereby economic logic and models seek to colonise sociological, anthropological, or political domains albeit that they are faced with resistance. Third is the homogenisation of theory, where a singular model of human behaviour is applied across contexts irrespective of historical, cultural, or structural differences. This echoes critiques of 'mono-economics' and the inappropriate application to low- and middle-income countries of theory derived for the GN (Hirschman, 1981; 1982; Myrdal, 1957; Seers, 1963).

In relation to the framing continuum, neo-classical thinking tends to present development as a matter of efficient allocation and incremental reform, system fixing rather than transformation. On the scope continuum, neo-classical economic imperialism promotes universalism, treating all countries as essentially the same in terms of economic logic, and thus diminishing the relevance of historical or positional differences between the Global North and South. Onto-epistemologically, neo-classical economics remain firmly positivist, prioritising quantification, deductive reasoning, and a narrowly defined objectivity.

A related but fourth distinct development in the social sciences has been the expansion of institutionalist thinking, which spans economics, political science, and sociology. New institutional economics (North, 1990), historical institutionalism (Mahoney and Thelen, 2010), and sociological institutionalism (Hall and Taylor, 1996) each emphasise the role of institutions, formal rules, informal norms, and organisational practices. And that it is these institutions that shape outcomes. These perspectives differ in focus: while new institutional economics retains a neo-classical rational-choice logic, historical and sociological institutionalism place greater emphasis on path dependency, ideas, and context. Across these variants, institutions are seen not merely as background 'conditions' but as active and often contested arenas in which development is negotiated.

In terms of the framing continuum, institutionalist perspectives vary: some support reformist agendas of institutional 'fixing', while others emphasise deeper transformation. On the scope continuum, institutionalist thinking often retains a comparative lens that acknowledges diversity across countries, though not necessarily in a North/South binary. Onto-epistemologically, institutionalist approaches span a spectrum, from positivist to constructivist, depending on disciplinary lineage and methodological preferences.

The emergence of Development Studies is shaped by, and remains entangled with, wider social science currents. The rise of post-structuralist and constructivist thought has challenged foundational assumptions about development knowledge, while the persistence of neo-classical economic imperialism has reinforced universalist, market-centric paradigms and fed resistance to them in Development Studies. These intellectual trends have not only diversified Development Studies but have also contributed to its fragmentation. Together, these shifts have influenced Development Studies as a field in which multiple, often competing modes of thought co-exist. The next section turns to examine how Development Studies has navigated these currents through its core characteristic of cross-disciplinarity.

2.3 Cross-Disciplinarity

Few scholars view Development Studies as a traditional discipline. Disciplines are typically defined by a relatively stable set of core concepts, foundational theories, and standardised methods, even if there is some contestation within. Development Studies, by contrast, lacks a unified conceptual or methodological canon. Instead, it is better understood as a cross-disciplinary field that draws selectively from a range of social science disciplines without fully replicating or fully integrating any of them. This cross-disciplinary nature is one of its strengths, but also a source of persistent tension and fragmentation in Development Studies.

Understanding these discussions in Development Studies requires engaging with the broader literature on what constitutes a discipline. Krishnan (2009) offers a multi-dimensional analysis of academic disciplines, examining them through philosophical, sociological, anthropological, historical, and managerial lenses. He argues that disciplines are not fixed categories, but socially constructed systems of knowledge production and professional organisation. From a philosophical perspective, Krishnan charts the evolution from Enlightenment ideals of unified science to post-structuralist critiques emphasising incommensurability and epistemic pluralism. Sociologically, disciplines are viewed as institutionalised communities with shared norms and division of intellectual labour, which reproduce their authority through mechanisms of professionalisation and academic gatekeeping. Anthropologically, disciplines resemble 'tribes' with distinct languages, rituals, and boundaries, features that foster cohesion but can also discourage collaboration. Historically, disciplines evolve unevenly, with newer fields lacking the prestige or autonomy of older disciplines. Finally, from a managerial perspective, disciplines are shaped by institutional incentives, audit cultures, and the marketisation of higher education. Interdisciplinarity may be idealised, but as Krishnan notes, it remains structurally and culturally difficult to achieve.

This difficulty is clearly visible in Development Studies. While the field aspires to draw on multiple disciplines, the integration of disciplinary insights is uneven overall and often asymmetric. Some schools of thought in Development Studies are more dominated by economics, others by anti-economics sentiments, others by anthropology or sociology; still others attempt to mix disciplines more thoroughly, but often face onto-epistemological tensions in doing so. In this context, the field cannot be neatly characterised as deep interdisciplinary. Rather, it may be better described as exhibiting multidisciplinarity, that is, the co-existence of multiple disciplinary perspectives without full integration or a shallower form of interdisciplinarity where there is a clearly dominant discipline in the mix. This unevenness also reflects the currents in the social sciences discussed in the previous section. The rise of post-structuralism has encouraged epistemic divergences and suspicion of grand theory. Meanwhile, the spread of neo-classical economic imperialism, and resistance to it, has pulled Development Studies both towards and away from positivist approaches.

A useful empirical lens on the question of cross-disciplinarity in Development Studies is provided by Mitra et al. (2020), who analysed citation patterns in several Development Studies journals over the period 1990–2018. Their dataset included field-specific journals such as World Development, Development and Change, and The Journal of Development Studies. It also included journals like The Journal of Human Development and Capabilities (often viewed as tied to the Capability Approach developed by Amartya Sen) and Development Policy Review (which focuses more on policy than traditional academic journals). Despite such caveats, the study's findings are telling: citation exchanges between Development Studies and other social sciences are limited, particularly beyond the domain of development economics. Most cross-disciplinary citation occurred within a relatively narrow loop: development economics, economics more broadly, and the core Development Studies journals. Cross-citations with political science and geography although increased modestly, especially after the mid-2000s, but remained limited.

These findings support a more sceptical reading of interdisciplinarity in Development Studies. While there is rhetorical commitment to disciplinary integration, in practice the field often remains siloed, particularly when it comes to integrating disciplines with deeply contrasting ontological and epistemological assumptions, such as economics and anthropology. The growing presence of economists in Development Studies journals may not reflect deeper interdisciplinarity. It may reflect a shifting publication strategy by economists facing greater competition in economics journals, particularly given the rise of microeconomics as the dominant subfield.

Clarifying what is meant by different forms of cross-disciplinarity is therefore important. Cross-disciplinarity is often used as an umbrella term, encompassing three distinct modes: multidisciplinarity, interdisciplinarity, and transdisciplinarity. As Molteberg and Bergstrøm (2000) argue, these modes represent increasing levels of integration. Multidisciplinary research brings together perspectives from different disciplines but retains their boundaries. Interdisciplinary research seeks to synthesise or integrate disciplinary tools, concepts, or methods but is a range from shallow to deep intergration. Transdisciplinary research, the most ambitious form, seeks to transcend disciplinary boundaries altogether. A related concept is non-disciplinarity, which refers to a deliberate avoidance or rejection of disciplinary frameworks altogether.

George (2025) discusses distinctions, drawing on Klein (2017). The review highlights the persistent ambiguity in terminology, as well as the structural and professional barriers that hinder integrated collaboration. While interdisciplinary and transdisciplinary research are often lauded for their innovation, relevance, and visibility, they remain under-supported in institutional terms. Career incentives, peer review mechanisms, and funding structures still favour disciplinary orthodoxy. As George notes, aligning the type of cross-disciplinary collaboration with the specific goals of a research project is crucial, and in many cases, 'multiple disciplinary' may be the most appropriate and accurate descriptor.

Kanbur (2002) makes a similar argument, contending that while full interdisciplinarity may be ideal, it is often unattainable in practice. Different disciplines rest on fundamentally different assumptions about ontology (what exists) and epistemology (what can be known). For example, a constructivist anthropologist and a positivist economist may have radically different views on causality, objectivity, and generalisability. Collaboration is easier when disciplines share some compatible assumptions. Consequently, cross-disciplinary research may require relaxing certain disciplinary assumptions, which can dilute the theoretical rigour or methodological coherence of the contributing disciplines.

These challenges are not merely intellectual. The persistence of strong institutional and professional barriers between disciplines reflects the way disciplines are organised and reproduced. Disciplines structure career paths, peer networks, funding applications, and publishing venues. As Abbott (2002) observes, academic identity is closely tied to disciplinary affiliation, and crossing disciplinary boundaries can feel unsettling. This tension is acutely felt by those in Development Studies, where many researchers trained in core disciplines may feel marginalised in their original disciplinary 'home', while also struggling to be accepted in other disciplines. In this sense, Development Studies has become a partial refuge for scholars whose research falls between disciplinary boundaries but not always of recognition outside of Development Studies.

The politics of disciplinarity also warrant attention. Turner (2000) argues that fields become disciplines when they secure identity through recognised departments or institutes and exchange through organised labour markets that reproduce graduates and staff via postgraduate training. Development Studies shows elements of both. It is offered at postgraduate level in over 150 universities worldwide, and many institutions have dedicated centres or departments, although not always under the label 'Development Studies'. Even where such structures exist, many faculty do not necessarily identify as Development Studies scholars or hold formal training in the field. Turner also describes disciplines as 'cartels' organised markets for training and employment with exclusionary tendencies. Development Studies exhibits some cartel-like features, yet its porous boundaries weaken exclusionary effects. Patterns of disciplinary dominance nonetheless persist, with economics particularly influential in some schools of thought, while anthropology and sociology are more prominent in decolonial or postcolonial approaches.

These disciplinary imprints correspond closely with the three continua of this book. In terms of the framing continuum, some disciplines may have a tendency to favour technocratic or reformist understandings of development, while other disciplines may lean towards systemic transformation or critique. On scope, some constituent disciplines tend to promote universalist assumptions. Others tend to stress historical specificity and the structural distinctiveness of the Global South. Finally, the onto-epistemological continuum is perhaps the most salient: economics remains largely positivist and deductive, while other disciplines adopt constructivist or critical realist positions.

In short, Development Studies is not a discipline but a cross-disciplinary field shaped by tensions, trade-offs, and negotiations between often incompatible disciplinary logics. Its openness is both a strength and a source of instability. The ideal of interdisciplinarity is frequently cited but rarely realised; multidisciplinarity is more common or shallower forms of interdisciplinarity. Meanwhile, transdisciplinarity remains largely aspirational. The consequences of these dynamics are significant: the framing, scope, and epistemological premises of development research vary dramatically depending on the often-dominant discipline. The next section turns to discuss further how these diverse and often incompatible knowledge foundations manifest within Development Studies, and how they underpin competing modes and schools of thought.

2.4 Contemporary Development Studies

2.4.1 Knowledge Foundations

To engage meaningfully with the differentiation and cross-disciplinarity of Development Studies, it is useful to examine the foundational components of knowledge that underlie diverse modes of inquiry within the field. Bevan's

(2007) concept of 'knowledge foundations' provides a systematic framework for this analysis, enabling a structured interrogation of how different epistemic communities, within and beyond Development Studies, construct, validate, and apply knowledge. Bevan's foundations of knowledge are useful in thinking about differentiation within Development Studies as they were developed to do so with a focus on poverty and illbeing/wellbeing in Bevan's own research (see e.g., 2003; 2004a; 2004b; 2005). This section uses Bevan's approach to unpack ontological, epistemological, methodological, and normative diversity in Development Studies. It also sets the stage for Sections 4b and 4c, where we consider the field's conceptual continua and its divergent schools of thought.

Bevan's framework can be usefully organised into three interrelated domains. The first relates to the focus or problematic of inquiry: What is the research concerned with, and why? This encompasses values, ideology, and standpoint, often implicit in disciplinary traditions, that shape research priorities. The second domain concerns the ontological and epistemological assumptions of inquiry: What is the world assumed to be like, and how can it be known? This includes theories, conceptual models, and explanatory frameworks. The third domain relates to research strategies, methodologies, instruments, and modes of analysis: How is empirical knowledge generated, and for what purpose is it used? These domains also encompass questions of praxis, including how knowledge is disseminated and by whom.

This three-part structure helps capture the diversity and complexity of Development Studies. Unlike many social science disciplines that coalesce around relatively stable concepts and theories, Development Studies operates at the intersection of disciplines that differ markedly in their epistemic assumptions, methodological preferences, and normative commitments. This hybridity presents both strengths and challenges: while cross-disciplinarity enables conceptual innovation in principle, it also creates tensions around coherence, legitimacy, and rigour. Indeed, each discipline, and often subdiscipline, operates with core concepts that are treated as largely unproblematic within its own community but become contested when applied elsewhere as Bevan notes. For example, disciplines are often embedded in normative visions of the 'good life', each with distinct views on progress and development. These visions shape the values and assumptions that underpin knowledge production, especially in a normative field like Development Studies. Ontological assumptions, about what constitutes social reality, also vary across disciplines, ranging from the structural to the interpretive and from the material to the discursive.

At the heart of Bevan's schema is a fundamental divide between positivist and relativist epistemologies, a demarcation that mirrors broader currents in the social sciences discussed earlier in this chapter. The positivist tradition, dominant in economics and segments of political science, foregrounds empirical regularities, statistical analysis, and causal inference. It assumes an objective reality that can be known through observation and generalisation. By contrast, relativist and constructivist perspectives, more prominent in anthropology, sociology, and geography, argue that reality is socially constructed, multiple, and historically contingent. These approaches prioritise interpretation, meaning-making, and the role of language and power in shaping knowledge. Critical realism offers a middle ground. Bhaskar (1979) acknowledged an independent reality while distinguishing between 'the real' (structures and mechanisms), 'the actual' (events that occur), and 'the empirical' (observable experiences). It favours methodological pluralism and emphasises the explanatory adequacy of theoretical claims, rather than their verification through direct observation.

These epistemological differences give rise to a plurality of research strategies. Namely, as Blaikie (1993) identifies, there are: inductive (deriving theory from empirical observation), deductive (testing pre-existing theory), abductive (deriving insights from actors' meanings), and retroductive (inferring the underlying mechanisms of social phenomena). Further, across Development Studies, all four strategies are evident. Bevan also draws on Mouzelis (1995) to distinguish among different conceptions of theory: as conceptual frameworks, sets of propositions, or scaffolding for further theorisation. Bevan (2007) further proposes a view of theory as a 'structure of being' across time and space. This includes its 'anatomy' (the components and relationships within a system), 'physiology' (the regular processes that sustain it), 'dynamics' (the mechanisms of change and stability), and 'histories' (the contextualised trajectories of real-world instances). This conceptualisation offers a richer, diachronic understanding of theoretical work, particularly useful in Development Studies, where temporality, contingency, and multiplicity are important.

The diversity of methodological preferences across disciplines further complicates cross-disciplinary engagement. Most economists privilege large-N datasets and regression analysis; anthropologists, by contrast, often favour ethnographic methods and 'thick description'. Political scientists focus on institutional analysis, while geographers explore spatial relationality. These disciplinary traditions reflect different logics of explanation, ranging from causal generalisation to narrative understanding, and different modes of comparison. Bevan invokes Tilly's (1984) typology of comparative strategies, including individualising, universalising, variation-finding, and case-specific analysis, as ways in which researchers draw conclusions about development. These differences also shape the forms of rhetorical authority employed across disciplines, whether mathematical formalism, conceptual clarity, or narrative richness.

Taken together, Bevan's framework provides an analytical lens through which to assess differentiation within Development Studies. It allows us to formulate a series of diagnostic questions: What is the central 'problematic' of the research? Whose values and interests are privileged? What kinds of development (and for whom) are considered desirable or undesirable? These questions also resonate with the framing continuum. Further questions concern the assumed ontology and epistemology: What is social reality understood to be? How can it be known, and what kinds of evidence are privileged? These concerns map directly onto the third continuum. Finally, Bevan's focus on research strategies and praxis links to the continuum of scope: Which countries are included in Development Studies? Are 'developed' countries studied in the same way as 'developing' ones, and what are the methodological implications of this? What levels of analysis, local, national, regional, global, are prioritised? And who ultimately uses this knowledge, and to what ends? Bevan's knowledge foundations offer a way to map differentiation in Development Studies and relate it to debates on disciplinarity, epistemology, and the politics of knowledge. This provides a bridge to Section 4b, where we turn to the three continua of framing, scope, and onto-epistemology in Development Studies in greater depth.

2.4.2 Modes of Thought in Development Studies: Framing, Scope, and Onto-Epistemology

In order to move from a discussion of knowledge foundations to a typology of differentiation within Development Studies, it is useful to first consider how knowledge foundations translate into distinct *modes of thought* within the field. These can be broadly situated along three interrelated continua: the framing of development, the scope of development, and the onto-epistemological assumptions that underpin the study of development. Together, the continua account for cross-disciplinary heterogeneity and fragmentation and provide a framework for comparison.

The identification of these continua builds on earlier discussions of cross-disciplinarity and the inherent challenges of synthesising diverse disciplinary

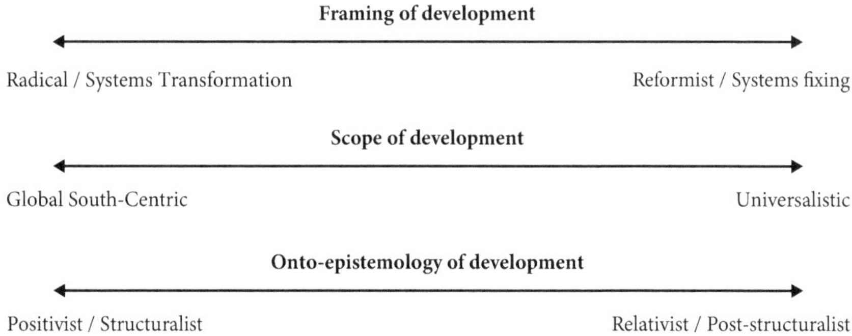

Figure 2.1 Modes of thought in Development Studies: Three Continua
Source: Author's elaboration.

assumptions, methodologies, and political-ideological orientations. The integration of disciplinary perspectives is rarely even or symmetrical, and the internal pluralism of Development Studies tends to coalesce into schools of thought that privilege different disciplinary lineages, often with limited mutual engagement. This results in intellectual silos which may reinforce the underlying assumptions, logics, and methods that shape both the production and use of knowledge. Figure 2.1 visually presents the continua.

The first axis of differentiation concerns the *framing* of development, that is, what development is understood to be, and what it is for. Some modes of thought conceive of development as a radical or transformative endeavour, aimed at fundamentally altering structures of inequality, domination, or exclusion. Others frame development as a more reformist project of systems maintenance, concerned with improving or stabilising existing arrangements. This continuum recalls Cox's distinction between 'problem-solving' and 'critical' theory in international relations (Cox, 1981). The former seeks to make the world function better within existing frameworks, while the latter aims to interrogate and potentially transcend those frameworks. In other words, problem-solving is aimed at 'systems maintenance' or fixing, rather than 'systems transformation' or the imagining of better worlds as critical theory does. In Development Studies, these divergent framings of development are not merely technical or programmatic. They are underpinned by different normative and ideological assumptions about what constitutes a 'better' world, and what role development thinking and practice should play in achieving it For illustration, Gore (2000) contrasts the early post-war vision of development as emancipation through structural transformation with later moves towards performance assessment, where progress is read off indicators. In subsequent time, he links this to a poverty-reduction paradigm shaped by quantifiable targets. The use of indicators is not apolitical, but a technocratic focus can obscure the structural and historical processes that critical approaches seek to foreground.

It is important to note that transformative framings of development are not monolithic. For some, such transformation may involve reclaiming the tradition of state-led development planning and structural transformation evident in the 1955 Bandung vision or in socialist development models. For others, it entails a more fundamental rupture with Western modernity, including a revaluation of epistemologies, values, and cosmologies rooted in the Global South. Thus, while both reformist and radical framings co-exist in Development Studies, they rest on very different assumptions about what the purpose of development should be and how it should or should not be pursued.

The second continuum addresses the *scope* of development, or more precisely, where and for whom development is seen to apply. This relates directly to long-standing debates about whether Development Studies should retain its historical focus on the Global South or whether it should instead adopt a more universalist perspective that includes global development challenges and dynamics in the Global North.

Historically, the field focused squarely on the newly independent nations of Africa, Asia, and Latin America. These countries were cast as 'developing' in contrast to the presumed 'developed' Global North, and this binary formed the foundational binary of Development Studies. Yet, recent contributions, from Horner and Hulme (2019a) and Leach et al. (2021; 2024), have questioned the continuing utility of this binary. Increasingly, issues such as inequality, climate change, migration, and precarity transcend North–South divides and demand a more universalist lens they argue. Such calls for universalism are not without critique. As Wiegratz et al. (2023) and others have argued, decentring the Global South risks flattening the historical and structural specificities of global inequality. The question is not merely empirical, i.e., whether poor people exist in the North as well as the South, but also analytical and normative: does development mean the same thing in the GN as it does in the GS? Seers' (1963) argument about the 'special case' of developing countries continues to resonate in this context, especially in light of enduring global hierarchies and asymmetries of power.

Thus, the scope continuum is not simply about geography but also about how historical legacies and global structures are conceptualised. Those who maintain a GS-centred perspective tend to emphasise colonial and neocolonial histories, the role of core-periphery relations in the world economy, and the continuing epistemic subordination of the South. Those with a universalist orientation, by contrast, tend to see development as a shared global condition shaped by interdependence, transnational flows, and systemic risks.

The third continuum concerns the *onto-epistemological* assumptions that underpin different approaches to the study of development. This encompasses assumptions about what social reality is (ontology), and how it can be known (epistemology). Different schools of thought in Development Studies adopt contrasting views along this axis, ranging from positivist or structuralist approaches to relativist or post-structuralist ones. Positivist approaches tend to privilege causal inference, hypothesis testing, and the use of quantitative methods to uncover objective truths about development outcomes. These approaches are often dominant in economics and political science and may resonate with the tradition of 'mono-economics' critiqued by Hirschman (1981; 1982). In contrast, post-structuralist and constructivist approaches emphasise interpretation, discourse, and the socially constructed nature of both development problems and solutions. These are more prominent in anthropology, sociology, and human geography. Critical realism, as noted, situated between these poles, offers an intermediary position by positing that an objective reality exists independently of our perceptions but that our access to it is mediated by social, historical, and discursive processes. This has led to a range of methodological innovations, such as retroduction and abduction noted earlier, which attempt to navigate between empiricist and interpretivist positions.

The onto-epistemological continuum also intersects with different understandings of power. Power may be understood materially, as rooted in economic structures, class relations, and global asymmetries, or epistemically, as embedded in discourse, knowledge regimes, and systems of representation. These divergent conceptions of power inform not only how oppression is theorised, but also what counts as valid knowledge and legitimate method. Whether researchers draw on Marx, Foucault, Fanon, or Acemoglu and Robinson reflects deeper assumptions about causality, agency, and justice.

These three continua, framing, scope, and onto-epistemology, provide a heuristic for mapping differentiation within Development Studies and clarifying how divergent knowledge foundations translate into competing research agendas. They also underscore the difficulties of cross-disciplinarity: while disciplines may be combined in individual studies or programmes, the foundational assumptions underpinning those disciplines often remain in tension, especially across the three continua. In this sense, the field's heterogeneity is not simply a matter of scholarly preference or methodological diversity, but reflects more profound divergences over meaning, purpose, and politics. As the following Section will show, schools of thought in Development Studies can be situated along these continua, revealing how combinations of framing, scope, and onto-epistemology give rise to distinctive, and sometimes incommensurable, modes and schools of thought.

2.4.3 Comparison of Exemplar Schools of Thought in Development Studies

The contemporary landscape of Development Studies is marked by the coexistence of several distinct schools of thought. These schools can be compared and contrasted in terms of their positions on the three continua outlined. These are the framing of development (transformative or reformist), the scope of development (Global South-focused or universalist), and the onto-epistemological foundations (positivist/structuralist or relativist/poststructuralist). Each school reflects different disciplinary leanings, normative commitments, and modes of theorising development, as well as diverging assumptions about the nature and mechanisms of power and oppression.

An important observation concerns the disciplinary compositions underpinning these schools of thought. Some tend to draw primarily on economics and political science, often with an emphasis on material power relations, institutions, and political economy structures. Others lean more heavily into sociology, anthropology, and geography thereby engaging more directly with discursive constructions, cultural hegemony, and epistemic power. These disciplinary differences inform the divergent understandings of what constitutes the primary mechanisms of oppression in global development, whether these are to be found in material structures of exploitation or in the politics of knowledge and representation. To reiterate, epistemic power, as previously outlined, is rooted in discourses, ideas, and symbolic domination. Scholars working within this argue that the marginalisation of non-Western knowledge systems, the stereotyping and essentialisation of the 'Other', and the reproduction of colonial logics through development discourse constitute the dominant oppressive mechanisms shaping development outcomes. Knowledge, in this view, is not merely descriptive or analytical, but deeply political and implicated in the reproduction of global hierarchies. Conversely, those working within the tradition of materialist political economy locate oppression more squarely in structural inequalities, global economic relations, and the institutional arrangements that reproduce these. Here, power is exercised through concrete relations, of trade, finance, production, debt, and ownership, that are embedded in and shaped by the international political economy.

Table 2.1 summarises the four exemplar schools of thought discussed in this section and locates each across the three continua of framing, scope, and onto-epistemology. It presents a comparison of their primary focus and purpose, disciplinary anchors, and perspective on power, to show where the schools align and where they diverge. What follows is a comparative overview of four major schools of thought within Development Studies, each of which can be situated along the framing, scope, and onto-epistemological continua discussed. While ideal-typical, these schools are not rigid or mutually exclusive. They are dynamic and internally heterogeneous, and there is often movement across boundaries, hybridisation, and dialogue at the margins. We discuss each in turn.

A first school may be termed *Classical Development Studies*. This approach corresponds to what might be called the foundational phase of Development Studies, rooted in the post-war decades of the 1940s/1950s through the 1960s/1970s, and strongly influenced by classical development economics and political economy. Its framing of development is transformative, aiming for large-scale structural transformation of economies and societies through industrialisation and state-led development planning. This school is typically situated at the Global South end of the scope continuum. It emerged in response to the particular challenges of 'late development' in postcolonial contexts and remains centred on the specific structural disadvantages faced by countries in the South. The emphasis on national development strategies, import substitution industrialisation (ISI), and the strategic role of the developmental state reflects this situatedness. Onto-epistemologically, this school aligns more with more positivistic leaning traditions. While not wholly divorced from historical contingency and context, it tends to assume the existence of objective development constraints and causal mechanisms that can be diagnosed and addressed through theory-informed empirical analysis. Influential scholars such as Chang (1994a, 1994b, 2002), Wade (1990), and others working in the tradition of Latin American structuralism and dependency theory, such as Furtado (e.g. 1964; 1965), Prebisch (e.g. 1950), and Sunkel (e.g. 1966), are representative of this tradition. Development, in this view, is hampered by external dependency, structural asymmetries in global trade and production. These are challenges to be overcome, rather than naturalised or reproduced. The analytical lens of this school is often historical-institutional and grounded in political economy.

Table 2.1 Comparison of Schools of Thought in Development Studies

School of Thought	Primary Focus	Purpose	Dominant Disciplines	View of Power	Framing of Development	Scope of Development	Onto-Epistemology
Classical Development Studies	Industrialisation, national development strategies, structural transformation	To identify constraints to late development and design national strategies for structural change	Development economics, political economy, historical sociology	Material (structural constraints, global hierarchy)	Transformative (systems transformation, structural change)	Global South-centred (late development, structural disadvantage)	Structuralist, positivist; some critical realist elements
Problem-Solving Development Studies	Aid, conflict resolution, poverty reduction, institutional reform	To improve aid delivery, programme design, and institutional performance through evidence-based policy	Development economics, public policy, IR, conflict studies	Institutional and structural (state fragility, governance, aid effectiveness)	Reformist (systems fixing, institutional capacity)	Global South-centred (low-income, fragile, conflict-affected states)	Positivist, instrumental rationality
Post-Development and Decolonial Studies	Knowledge hierarchies, resistance, alternatives to development, pluriversality	To challenge dominant paradigms, empower subordinated knowledges, and build pluriversal alternatives	Anthropology, sociology, philosophy, postcolonial theory	Epistemic/discursive (representation, knowledge production, coloniality)	Transformative (critique of capitalist modernity and development discourse)	Universalist (global discursive domination, epistemic violence)	Post-structuralist, constructivist, relativist, pluriversal
Global Development Studies	Global challenges, convergence/divergence, SDGs, inequality across all countries	To understand global interconnections and generate knowledge across national boundaries	geography, environmental studies, political economy, public policy studies	Structural and relational (inter-dependence, global systems, complexity)	Reformist (systems adaptation, planetary inter-dependence)	Universalist (development as global across North and South)	Mixed

Source: Author.

A second school of thought is what may be termed *Problem-Solving Development Studies*. This school gained prominence in the 1990s and beyond and is marked by its reformist orientation, Global South focus, and tendency towards more positivistic leaning epistemologies. As noted in earlier work (Sumner, 2022; 2024), this school can also be labelled 'aid-dependence framed Development Studies' or 'aid-fragility-conflict Development Studies'. Drawing on Cox's (1981) distinction between critical and problem-solving theory, this school operates within the existing order. Its central concern is how to improve outcomes, poverty reduction, conflict mitigation, service delivery, within prevailing institutional and policy frameworks. Development is framed not as a transformative societal project but as incremental progress, often defined in terms of measurable outcomes such as health, education, or GDP per capita.

The disciplinary foundations of this school are mixed but include a strong influence from development economics, public policy, and international relations. It often draws on quantitative methods and 'evidence-based' policy tools. Knowledge is treated as cumulative, and the focus is often on finding 'what works' through the use of evaluations, and indicator-driven analysis.

Geographically, the school tends to focus on 'fragile states', countries that are highly aid-dependent and afflicted by conflict or institutional weaknesses. Development is viewed as possible, though difficult, and is often seen as dependent on external support. It is in this school that the legacy of 'Northern-perceived' problems of the Global South is most visible: concerns about migration, terrorism, or pandemics drive interventions that are rationalised through the lens of global public goods or donor interests. The role of aid is central, though not uncritically embraced.

In sum, the school of 'Problem Solving' Development Studies works within the existing order to make existing institutions work better to address problems rather than question the prevailing order and/or the social forces underlying it. Problem-solving Development Studies prioritises incremental improvement within existing institutions. It often concentrates on fragile or aid-dependent contexts and employs evaluation-centred evidence to inform programmes (see, for example, Bizhan, 2022; MacGinty and Williams, 2016; Carment and Samy, 2023). This school could be recast as 'targeted' Development Studies, using the term of Bermeo (2018) who refers to 'targeted development' to refer to donor self-interests such as how migration, security, or disease control shapes aid allocation and policies. The empirical focus then narrows to programme delivery and measurable outputs. Whatever the label, in some sense, there is a dimension that this school is often Northern-perceived problems of the Global South. This school reflects a narrowing of Development Studies in both scope and ambition. The transformative aspirations of the classical tradition are replaced by the pursuit of improved service delivery in settings where fundamental change is seen as infeasible or undesirable. In this sense, problem-solving Development Studies is emblematic of what Gore (2000) called the 'performative' turn in development thinking.

The third school is a broad and internally diverse constellation encompassing *post-development*, *postcolonial*, and *decolonial* perspectives. While this family of thought emerged in earnest in the 1990s, its intellectual antecedents stretch back further and include anti-colonial critiques and radical epistemologies from the Global South. It is positioned at the radical-transformation end of the framing continuum, is more universalist in scope, and is characterised by post-structuralist or constructivist onto-epistemologies.

The school represents a wide range of intellectual positions. The original post-development thinking (e.g., Escobar, 1992; Esteva, 1985; 1992; Rahnema, 1997) has been developed further in by postcolonial and decolonial theorists (for a range of discussions, see Bhambra, 2014; Grosfoguel, 2007; Kothari et al., 2019; Mignolo, 2002; 2021; Quijano, 2007; Lugones, 2007; Ndlovu-Gatsheni, 2018; 2020; Okoth, 2023; Pailey, 2020; Patel, 2020; Wilson, 2012). Some premises of the school of thought draw on Foucault's (1970; 1972; 1977; 1980; 1991) and Said's (1978; 1983; 1993) thinking as flagged earlier, namely that the North's political and intellectual depictions of the 'Third World' have been essential to subordinating the latter by 'plunder and violence' (Alvares, 1992, p. 1) or that the construction of the Global South as 'inferior' to developed countries is considered to serve as justification for subordination by the North.

This school represents perhaps the most forceful challenge to the foundational assumptions of development thinking. It critiques not only the outcomes of development but the very idea of development itself as a Eurocentric, hierarchical, and modernist discourse. Foundational texts such as those noted above, namely, Escobar (1995), Esteva (1992), and Rahnema (1997) argue that 'development' has served as a mechanism of domination, reinforcing the geopolitical, cultural, and epistemological hegemony of the North. The school's definition of development is then more about what is not desirable, namely capitalist modernity in part or whole.

The school generally challenges or repudiates the entire or many components of capitalist modernity and the pursuit of development in its current form though some may discuss different modernities, and different ways capitalism presents itself (e.g., Echeverría, 1995 and debate with Dussel, 2015). Development as widescale Western-type modernisation is deemed impossible and undesirable for the Global South. The 'rhizomatic' concept from Deleuze and Guattari (1980) helps explain how this school challenges linear, hierarchical, universal, and binary modes of thinking. It is also critical of traditional development theory that assumes a Eurocentric hierarchy of knowledge and the dominance of Western theory. 'Rhizomatic' contrasts with 'arborescent' or tree-like structures that have clear origins, roots, and branches and follow fixed logic. Rhizomatic structures have no single origin, no central tree trunk, and no direction predetermined. In particular, Rhizomatic structure resists linear causality.

To conceptualise alternatives to capitalist modernity, Garcia-Arias et al. (2024) extend the rhizomatic concept and propose the concept of a 'rhizomatic pluriverse'. This concept, they argue, interconnects the diverse alternative modes of existence and cognition in a decentralised, non-hierarchical system. They utilise Andean philosophy and networks and illustrates the 'Global Tapestry of Alternatives'. This thus sits in contrast to universalist models of progress in advocating for *pluriversality*, the recognition of multiple, co-existing ways of knowing and being. The 'rhizomatic pluriverse' exemplifies this ethos: knowledge is seen as non-linear, non-hierarchical, and locally grounded. Development is reconceived not as a singular trajectory but as a multiplicity of context-specific alternatives, often drawing on Indigenous knowledges, feminist epistemologies, and radical ecological thought.

In Development Studies, this school is thus a challenge to any linear models of progress or universal approaches or models of development or frameworks to understand development or fixed prescriptions. The school also challenges traditional development theory that assumes a Eurocentric hierarchy of knowledge and the dominance of Western theory. It advocates 'pluriversal' approaches, or multiple, co-existing ways of knowing and context-specific understandings, emphasising the fluid, adaptive nature of development (Escobar, 1995; Garcia-Arias et al., 2024; Rist, 2008).

A defining feature of this school is its privileging of epistemic power. Development is not simply a policy or economic process but a discursive regime that constructs the South as deficient and in need of external intervention. Drawing on Foucault, Said, Spivak, and others, post-development and decolonial scholars interrogate how knowledge systems naturalise hierarchies, how 'expertise' is used to justify intervention, and how categories such as 'underdevelopment' are socially constructed. The school also highlights the oppression of the GS by the GN as well as epistemic power and questions of race (see for discussion Escobar 1995; Garcia-Arias et al., 2024; Rist 2008; and related to pluriversality, de la Cadena and Blaser, 2018; Garcia-Arias et al., 2025; Gills and Hosseini, 2022; Kothari et al., 2019). This school seeks to 'unlearn' development as a colonial project and to promote alternatives arising from the lived experiences of subordinated groups. The scope is universal in that power and domination are seen as global phenomena, but the emphasis is on amplifying Southern perspectives and undoing the hierarchies that structure knowledge production.

The fourth school is what may be termed *Global Development Studies*. This school can be traced to debates from the 1970s, and later to globalisation studies. It explores differences between national development problems and cross-border or global interdependencies (Currie-Alder, 2016) and what they mean for the study of development. Global Development Studies is reformist leaning in framing, universal in scope, and sits somewhere in the middle of the onto-epistemological continuum, drawing on both positivist and interpretivist approaches. As noted, it has been the subject of discussion since the 1970s (see de Haan and Maxwell, 1998; Gaventa, 1998; Mehta et al., 2006; Saith, 2006; Seers et al., 1979) and has garnered particular interest following Horner and Hulme (2019a; 2019b), Leach et al. (2021; 2024), and Oldekop et al. (2020), though with critical responses (e.g., Alemany et al., 2019; Bangura, 2019; Büscher, 2019; Fischer, 2019; Ghosh, 2019; Hope et al., 2022; Onaran, 2019; Ziai, 2019; Wiegratz et al., 2023).

The school challenges the long-standing binary between 'developed' and 'developing' countries, arguing that such distinctions have become increasingly untenable. Instead, it posits that development issues, poverty, inequality, climate change, urbanisation, are now global in nature and must be studied as such. The analytical scope of this school is thus expansive, encompassing both North and South, and emphasising interdependence, transnational challenges, and planetary boundaries. It stresses the interconnectedness of development outcomes and seeks to understand how global trends shape national and local trajectories. While this universalism is appealing to some, critics argue that it risks flattening the field, eliding the structural inequalities and historical legacies that continue to shape the Global South (see e.g., Wiegratz et al., 2023).

These four schools of thought illustrate the contemporary differentiation within Development Studies. Each occupies a place across the three continua of framing, scope, and onto-epistemology, and each carries its own intellectual heritage and normative commitments. Yet, as argued in these positions are not fixed. Scholars may shift across boundaries, blend approaches, and engage in dialogue. More fundamentally, these schools exemplify the broader tensions of Development Studies as a cross-disciplinary field. They reflect not only differing theories of development but divergent ways of knowing, different assumptions about social reality, and alternative visions of justice and change. As such, Development Studies is not a unified field but a terrain of contestation. Dow (2002) argued that the plurality of modes of thought within economics should be seen as epistemologically legitimate alternatives rather than aberrations from a norm. Similarly, Development Studies houses divergent worldviews and methodological commitments that are not reducible to a Kuhnian paradigm of normal science. Instead, Development Studies operates within what Dow would see as a pluralist intellectual ecosystem, where coherence within a mode does not preclude cross-mode dialogue but does complicate it. Thus, rather than a crisis in the Kuhnian sense, Development Studies may be better understood as experiencing a splintering into semi-autonomous, co-existing modes of thought, each with its own problematiques, analytical vocabularies, and normative commitments. Like Dow's analysis of economics, this points to the need for more active engagement across difference.

2.5 Conclusion

This chapter has explored the intellectual architecture of Development Studies through engagement with currents in social science, the challenges of cross-disciplinarity, and the foundations of knowledge. The discussion has built on the preceding debates to propose a conceptual framework for understanding differentiation within Development Studies. This is structured around three continua of framing, scope, and onto-epistemology. This framework enables a more systematic comparison of the diverse modes of thought that co-exist within the field.

As the chapter has shown, Development Studies comprises a set of co-existing but often non-communicating modes of thought. These knowledge communities are shaped by differing assumptions about what constitutes development, where it occurs, and how it should be understood or known. These communities are often sustained by partial alignments with particular disciplines. Their internal logics are structured by distinct combinations of normative orientations, theoretical commitments, methodological practices, and epistemic sensibilities. Some privilege structural explanations rooted in political economy. Others foreground discursive and epistemic constructions of development. Some seek reformist change within existing systems. Others imagine and advocate for radical transformation.

These distinctions are not simply abstract differences. They are embodied in research outputs, teaching curricula, institutional affiliations, and even in the allocation of funding and citation patterns. They are underpinned by contrasting responses to fundamental questions about the purpose of development, the role of the state, the agency of subaltern groups, the nature of knowledge, and the locus of authority in defining development pathways. The framework elaborated in this chapter, offers a way to make these differences more legible. In doing so, the chapter draws from and extends earlier critiques of paradigmatic closure in the social sciences. Kuhn's (1962) notion of paradigm shifts has been influential in understanding intellectual change. It fits poorly, however, where several non-hegemonic paradigms co-exist. Development Studies shows such pluralism closer to Dow's 'modes of thought' than to normal science. And each with its own internal coherence and methodological commitments. As Dow suggests in her work on economics, such modes are not necessarily commensurable but are nevertheless capable of yielding valid insights. The implication is not the celebration of diversity for its own sake, but the recognition that pluralism, if reflexively engaged with, can be a source of intellectual dynamism. Such pluralism also brings risks. There is a risk that different schools of thought speak past each other. The field may then lose its capacity to respond collectively to climate change, global inequality, geopolitical realignments, and the legitimacy crisis of aid and multilateralism. Further, the increasing differentiation within Development Studies may inhibit more cumulative knowledge-building or engagement between different modes of thought. The following chapters take forward this discussion by examining each continuum of differentiation in greater detail. They consider, respectively, the diverse framings of development, the contested scope of development inquiry, and the multiplicity of onto-epistemological foundations that underpin competing understandings of what development is, where it happens, and how it can be known.

3

Continuum I

The Framing of Development

Development and its Discontents. Andy Sumner, Oxford University Press. © Andy Sumner (2026).
DOI: 10.1093/9780198902904.003.0003

3.1 Introduction

In the previous chapter, we examined major intellectual shifts in the social sciences and their influence on the evolution of Development Studies. We then explored the foundational building blocks of knowledge in Development Studies, drawing on Bevan (2007), before turning to the modes of thought in Development Studies, and exemplar schools of thought. The discussion highlighted the tensions within Development Studies across the three continua outlined (framing, scope, onto-epistemology), which form the basis of the discussion of the remaining substantive chapters.

This chapter focuses on the framing of development, that is, whether development should entail a radical system transformation, in some manner, and to what extent it has been so in practice. At the other end of the continua on the framing of development is 'systems fixing' or 'systems maintenance', which involves more modest, reformist, stabilising, improving, refining, or fixing existing structures rather than pursuing radical change. The former, the notion of systems transformation, in development can take at least two broad forms. First, material reality and national economic development, typically associated with industrialisation, structural transformation, and the pursuit of modernity in keeping with emancipatory ideals of the Bandung conference. Second, an alternative societal transformation of discourse and what is valued moves away from economic measures towards cultural, social, or environmental assets. It may reject modernity and monetary valuation altogether, or draw on indigenous notions of value and wellbeing from the Global South. The latter (the notion of systems fixing) in development can take several forms too. Such as poverty reduction, peace-building or economic growth.

Applying Bevan's (2007) framework involves asking what Development Studies researchers study (focus, domain, or problematic of study) as well as why (values, standpoints, or ideology). The chapter argues that development can be understood as both a material process and outcome. It can also be a framing discourse with consequences for the material world. Each has intentional or willed and unintentional or unwilled aspects, drawing on Cowen and Shenton (1995; 1996) and on Hart (2001; 2002; 2010). For Cowen and Shenton, the dialectic is between immanent development, a historical process internal to capitalism and intentional development. The latter is a conscious project of improvement, usually pursued by the state or international agencies in policies, plans, and programmes. Cowen and Shenton argued that development always involves a tension between the two distinctions because development is a descriptive category or process and a prescriptive one too (a policy project). For Hart (2001; 2002; 2010), there is little 'd' and Big-'D' development. Big-'D' development refers to the post-Second World War project of organised development, encompassing aid programmes, multilateral institutions, national development planning, and the activities of NGOs. By contrast, little 'd' development denotes the wider processes of change bound up with capitalism, such as the restructuring of production, migration, agrarian transitions, and urbanisation. Hart's central argument is to shift attention from the doctrinal and trusteeship traditions highlighted in Cowen and Shenton to the historical conjuncture of the post-1945 geopolitical order. In this framing, Big D is an institutionalised project born out of that order.

In this chapter, it is argued though that there is a need to reclaim the notion of 'big-D' development, which is often dismissed as top-down, aid-driven, and oppressive though need not be so. Although Hart did not intend the Big-D/Small-d to be a binary, rather an interaction, there is a sense even in the original paper that Big-D is or was somehow 'bad' development. In an era where much of the Global South is post-ODA, ODA or 'aid' is no longer significant because domestic resources have grown. There is an opportunity to redefine big-D development as an emancipatory framing of development. This is the argument advanced in this chapter that development should entail radical and emancipatory systems transformation. This argument aligns with the anti-colonial aspirations of the Bandung Conference and the project of economic self-determination for the GS. One could argue that the economic transformation in the GS should be green, low-energy per capita or low carbon-based, in keeping with the climate risks the planet faces. However, one can argue back that it is for the Global North to reduce energy per capita use in order to allow the GS the option to pursue what the GN has had.

Why should development be transformational? A key argument is because incremental improvements alone, systems fixing, are insufficient to significantly alter life chances or a country's long-term trajectory even if there are some immediate improvements. As later data show, despite economic growth, large populations in post-ODA countries continue to live in or near absolute poverty. With the exception of a few cases, such as China, many GS countries remain structurally subordinated in the global economy. Moreover, the contemporary development model has further made national economic transformation subservient or secondary to the demands of the global economy, reinforcing dependence on external markets and finance rather than fostering 'deep' national economic development (of building entire industries). As a result, many ODA-dependent countries have barely begun the process of transformation. Most post-ODA countries face stalled economic development or even an 'early' deindustrialisation process. Here, 'early' means at a lower level of income or manufacturing share than the advanced nations achieved historically. We discuss these points further in this chapter.

The chapter is structured as follows: Section 2 discusses different conceptualisations of development and the evolution of this often-fierce debate over the core concept in DS. Section 3 seeks to ask, with much imperfection, what framings of development are evident within the GS. Section 4 examines the empirical record of development since the 1960s, assessing whether it has been transformational or not and why or why not. Section 5 concludes.

3.2 The Concept of Development

3.2.1 A Brief History

The core concept of DS, namely 'development', has long been a subject of heated debate within Development Studies accumulating multiple meanings and critiques over time. Since the field's emergence in the post-war era, competing theoretical perspectives have sought to define what constitutes development and how it should be pursued.

In the 1950s and 1960s, the dominant concern in Development Studies was economic transformation, particularly the structural shift from agrarian to industrial economies. Economists such as Furtado (1964; 1965), Lewis (1954), and Hirschman (1958) focused on strategies to promote industrialisation and national economic development in newly independent countries across Asia, sub-Saharan Africa, and also in long independent, Latin America. This emphasis on macroeconomic transformation, including policies aimed at reducing inequality between countries, was gradually displaced over subsequent decades by a stronger focus on social and human development, and poverty reduction.

The policy landscape of development has also shifted significantly over time. In the post-war decades, state-led development was central to economic planning, reflecting a commitment to sustained growth and material progress for broad segments of society. However, the neoliberal resurgence in the late 1970s and 1980s saw a retreat of the state as structural adjustment programmes in the GS promoted market-led development (Toye, 1987). During this period, discussions of industrialisation were pushed to the margins of development policy. Instead, the concept of development became associated with social and human development, first through the 'basic needs' approach (Streeten, 1979) and then through Sen's capability approach (1985; 1999), which emphasised expanding freedoms and investing in health and education. From the 1990s onward, framings of development expanded to include sustainability and governance. They remained within a human development paradigm, focused on rising incomes, capability expansion, and public good provision, rather than a productivist framework of structural transformation.

While mainstream development thinking has evolved, critical perspectives have sought to challenge the foundational assumptions on the necessity of material economic progress. Some scholars, notably those using a post-structrualist lens, argue that the conventional notion of development is rooted in Western ideals of modernity, reinforcing systemic global inequalities rather than addressing them (e.g., Mignolo, 2002; 2009; 2011; Rodney, 1972). Alternative perspectives advocate different forms of transformation. These include a redefinition of what is valued, 'alternative development' that seeks social and ecological change without capitalist modernity, and 'alternatives to development' that reject the premise of modernisation (Kothari et al., 2019; Lang and Mokrani, 2011; Nussbaum, 2011). These debates have gained further attention with calls for 'degrowth' and 'post-growth' approaches, which question the sustainability of continuous economic expansion (Jackson, 2009; Latouche, 2009). Degrowth has been debated in the Global North. It is often seen as less relevant to the GS, where development aspirations remain tied to economic expansion, especially in the poorest countries, though some discussions have questioned this (Acosta, 2013; Gudynas, 2011; Lang, 2017).

The meaning of development, therefore, remains inherently contested. Some define it as improving living standards, whether through economic growth or, more substantially, economic development, meaning industrialisation. Others prioritise human development, conceptualising development as the expansion of people's capabilities. In contrast, post-structuralists reject the very notion of 'development', viewing it as an ideological imposition of Western modernity on the Global South.

Looking back, the 1950s and 1960s vision of development at the independence of many GS countries was largely rooted in the economic transformation framing, aimed at the 'liberation' countries and people through national economic development (Gore, 2000, pp. 794–795). However, from the 1980s and 1990s, development was increasingly defined in 'performative' terms, meaning short-term metrics such as annual GDP growth, monetary poverty reduction, and basic needs indicators as noted above (e.g., primary school attendance or minimal income thresholds). This shift was though accompanied by, and critiqued by the emergence of post-development theorists, who drew on post-structuralist thought to argue that development is a discourse, a set of ideas that frame material reality and power relations (Escobar, 1992; 1995; Sachs, 1992). From this perspective, the 'development discourse' privileges Western modernity and the 'Western way of life', systematically portraying GS countries as lacking the economic assets necessary for development, and thus reinforcing a North–South hierarchy. Scholars such as Shiva (1993) have sought to redefine wealth by valuing cultural assets over economic ones, suggesting that even amid material poverty, the GS possesses significant cultural richness.

One common theme across all these perspectives is that development entails 'change' of some kind, though what kind of change, for whom, and who decides remain contentious questions. Chambers (2004, pp. 2–3) as noted earlier, offers a broad but influential definition: development as 'good change'. However, this definition immediately raises thorny issues (as Chambers readily acknowledged) on what is 'good' change, and who decides. Furthermore, should 'bad' change (such as environmental degradation or say rising inequality) be considered a form of development, even if framed as 'maldevelopment' or 'de-development' or 'underdevelopment? What is clear is that there is no single, uncontested definition of development that exists, nor is such a consensus ever likely to emerge. Kanbur (2006, p. 5) argues that, because values and ideas about the good life differ and, 'there is no uniform or unique answer'. This lack of consensus reflects divisions within Development Studies, where perspectives on development are often diametrically opposed on what is the core focus of the field.

3.2.2 Basic Principles

If we go back to basic principles, there are a set of fundamental distinctions across Development Studies in addition to the systems transformation versus systems fixing demarcation introduced in the Development Studies typology. First, there is a demarcation or rather an interaction between material versus non-material aspects in any framing of development. Second, a demarcation or an interaction between the intentional versus the unintentional aspects in a framing of development. Some scholars frame development as a material process and outcome, and intentional, emphasising structural transformation and socio-economic change. In contrast, others conceptualise development as a discourse, shaped by dominant ideas, values, and ideologies. Further, there is a distinction between intentional and unintentional development. Some approaches view development as a deliberate, state-led process, where elites (and/or perhaps aid donors in the poorest countries) seek to orchestrate economic and social transformation. Others emphasize spontaneous, unintentional transformations, shaped by broader historical, political, and economic forces rather than centralised planning. These distinctions highlight the diversity of interpretations within Development Studies, influencing how different schools of thought engage with the core concept of Development Studies, namely 'development'. Further, as pointed towards, these distinctions interact within themselves (i.e., intentional and unintentional development) and as well as between themselves. For example, state-led industrialisation reflects both an intentional and material conception of development. However, unintended consequences, such as increased inequality, can emerge even in planned development efforts.

A materialist approach sees development as a long-term historical process, typically involving the shift from agrarian to industrial production as previously noted (or more precisely a shift from the non-capitalist sector to the capitalist sector in keeping with Lewis (1954)). This transformation affects class structures, ownership patterns, and the organisation of production. By contrast, a discourse-based approach critiques development's ideological underpinnings, arguing that 'development' has reproduced Western hegemony rather than fostering genuine emancipation. Escobar, often cited as one originators of post-development theory, put it thus:

> Development was, and continues to be for the most part, a top-down, ethnocentric, and technocratic approach, which treated people and cultures as abstract concepts, statistical figures to be moved up and down in the charts of 'progress'. (Escobar, 1995, p. 44).

The modes of thought and schools of thought in Development Studies introduced in Chapter 2 reflect these conceptual differences. For example, Classical Development Studies views development as a material process, with a primary focus on national economic transformation. In contrast, Problem-Solving Development Studies tends to define development in performative terms, emphasising modest improvements in governance, conflict resolution, and poverty alleviation rather than large-scale structural change. Those scholars working in Post-Development/Post-Colonial/Decolonial Development Studies take a critical stance on development as a Western discourse imposed on the Global South, advocating for alternative conceptions of wellbeing and transformation that challenge the dominance of modernity. Finally, what has been labelled Global Development Studies adopts a broad, multidimensional approach, aligning development with universalistic frameworks such as the UN's Sustainable Development Goals (SDGs) that apply to all countries. In short, each of the schools frames development differently, leading to fundamentally divergent understandings of transformation, progress, and societal change within Development Studies.

A second distinction is whether the framing of development has more or less emphasis on the willed and orchestrated ('big-D' development) aspects or more or less emphasis on the organic, unplanned processes of development ('little-d' development) (drawing on Cowen and Shenton, 1995; 1996; Hart, 2001; 2002; 2010; see also review of Lewis, 2019). This also manifests different in each school. While critiques of Big-D development, particularly its links to Western imperial interests, are well-founded, not all intentional development is inherently problematic. The post-war success of East Asian economies, for instance, demonstrates that state-led transformation can be a GS-driven project, rather than merely an imposition of Northern models of development. In fact, as ODA becomes less significant to many GS economies, a vision of development, rooted in anti-colonial economic self-determination, would be Big-D development as a tool for GS-led transformation, rather than dismissed outright as inherently problematic.

The schools of Development Studies thus differ on these questions shaping their understandings of agency, power, planning, and the role of external actors. For example, Classical Development Studies emphasises the importance of development as a deliberate and strategic process, typically led by the state. Problem-Solving Development Studies emphasises development as intentional, but in a more incremental manner. Post-Development/Post-Colonial/Decolonial Development Studies largely rejects the notion of planned development, arguing that mainstream development efforts, particularly those orchestrated by the Global North, are hegemonic projects rather than genuine processes of emancipation. Instead, this school emphasises the importance of bottom-up transformations that emerge through resistance, alternative knowledge systems, and social movements. Finally, Global Development Studies tends to blend both intentional and unintentional dimensions of development, acknowledging top-down, policy-driven interventions while recognising that broader global shifts in economic structures, technology, environment, and social norms also shape development outcomes. These divergent perspectives on importance or problematic nature of the intentionality of development further illustrate the differences within Development Studies, influencing thinking on not only agency and power but on policy and the very feasibility of transformative change. The question thus arises of what framings of development are most evident in the Global South? Three potential answers can be explored, all of which are highly imperfect. Namely, national development plans, 'voices of the poor', and in indigenous concepts from the GS.

3.3 Framings of Development in the Global South

3.3.1 National Development Plans

Trying to address the question of what framings of development are most evident in the Global South is incredibly difficult (if not impossible) to answer. One can sketch a reply based on different sources. Each with limited representativeness. First, one way to approach it is through an elite-driven lens, examining how governments in the GS frame development in national development plans (NDPs). While this approach provides valuable insights, it primarily reflects the perspectives of political elites rather than the broader population. Nonetheless, it offers a useful entry point into the complexities of defining development. It is also inherently 'Big-D' development in emphasis.

Munro (2023) conducted a review of 140 GS countries' NDPs (and thirty high-income countries) from 2016 to 2023, focusing on the content of these plans. His findings indicate that in middle-income countries, themes of economic development and structural transformation, closer to classical Development Studies perspectives, are prominent. A broader study by Chimhowu et al. (2019) examined 107 NDPs, and provides further insight into the diversity of development framings across the Global South. Their analysis identifies a set of distinct categories of NDPs, each reflecting different approaches to the framing of development.

The first category is the largest component of the sample (40%) and is NDPs that were developed through participatory and broadbased processes. Potentially, these are the more representative NDPs (at least of those countries). These plans are typically developed through high levels of public engagement, integrating citizen input alongside expert analysis. They strike a balance between economic and social development objectives, frequently adopting the language of 'inclusive growth'. A second group of NDPs (20%) are participatory but weakly evidenced plans. These plans prioritise public consultation and accessibility, ensuring that development objectives reflect local voices and concerns. However, despite their participatory nature, they lack a strong empirical foundation to support effective implementation according to Chimhowu et al. Further, a third set of NDPs are 'expert-led plans' (25%). These plans are characterised by strong evidence base but limited social embeddedness, as they are primarily designed by technical experts with minimal public engagement. They focus predominantly on economic growth, trade, finance, and productivity. The remaining set of NDPs can be disregarded on quality grounds.[1]

In short, while almost a half of NDPs prioritise economic development, the largest share, 40%, adopts a mixed approach, balancing social and economic goals. The exercise shows the limits of seeking to identify a GS perspective on the question of the framing of development based solely on NDPs.

3.3.2 Participatory Assessments

While NDPs often reflect the perspectives of political elites, an alternative approach is to consider the views of marginalised populations, particularly those living in or near absolute poverty. One of the most notable attempts to capture these perspectives was the World Bank's 'Voices of the Poor' initiative, which was based on participatory research with 60,000 people across sixty countries in the late 1990s (Narayan et al., 2000a; 2000b). The fact that this was convened by the World Bank has made the findings contentious (see discussion of biases in Cornwall and Fujita, 2012). What the study did do was explore both material and non-material dimensions of poverty and underdevelopment. While economic deprivation was a central concern, participants also highlighted social exclusion and lack of power, daily humiliation and moral pain, and the persistent inequalities.

These findings suggest that, from the perspective of marginalised groups, development is not solely about material progress but also about dignity, agency, and social recognition. This perspective aligns with post-development/post-colonial/decolonial critiques somewhat, which challenge the assumption that modernity and economic growth necessarily equate to meaningful development. However, the research is now nearly thirty years old, raising questions about its contemporary relevance. Since the late 1990s, when this participatory assessment was conducted, many Global South (GS)

[1] Chimhowu et al. note that these NDPs were weakly structured and incoherent plans.

countries have experienced substantial rising incomes and poverty reduction, while others have seen little progress. These divergent trajectories complicate any attempt to generalise a singular GS perspective on development, underscoring the evolving and contested nature of the concept itself. An alternative presented by post-development/decolonial scholars is that of indigenous meanings of development from the Global South.

3.3c Indigenous Meanings: Buen Vivir, Ubuntu, and the Pluriverse

As part of the post-development/decolonial critique of modernity, a range of alternative, relational, and 'pluriversal' understandings of development have emerged, meaning a multiplicity of worlds, knowledges, and life practices that co-exist without seeking dominance or homogenisation. Among them, *Buen Vivir* in Latin America and *Ubuntu* in Africa are grounded in community, harmony, and ecological balance. The challenge with such meanings of development is to specify what they mean in practice and to assess how representativeness they are of views in the Global South.

Buen Vivir has become one of the most prominent alternatives proposed to 'development', particularly in Latin America. It offers not just a critique but a profound redefinition of development, understood not as economic accumulation but as collective wellbeing rooted in the reciprocity between humans, nature, and the cosmos. Emerging from Indigenous worldviews, *Buen Vivir* rejects the anthropo-centric and extractivist foundations of modern capitalism and instead proposes a bio- and cosmo-centric ethics grounded in harmony, relationality, and care (Lang, 2022; Gudynas, 2011). Garcia-Arias and Cuestas-Caza (2024) identify an 'intercultural, decolonial and ecological' form of *Buen Vivir*, deeply embedded in lived practices of Indigenous autonomies in Colombia, Ecuador, and Central America. Ideas such as *uywaña* and *uywanakuy*, mutual nurturing relations among humans and non-humans, illustrate a commitment to conviviality and care as central dimensions of wellbeing.

While *Buen Vivir* is firmly rooted in Latin American Indigenous traditions, *Ubuntu* emerges from African philosophy and serves as an articulation of development as human flourishing in communities. Typically, it is interpreted as 'I am, because we are; and since we are, therefore I am' (Mbiti, 1969, p. 108). *Ubuntu* situates individual wellbeing within the web of social relationships and shared humanity (Ramose, 1999). Development, from this perspective, cannot be separated from ethical and communal obligations, nor from the restoration of dignity and justice following histories of colonialism and dispossession. Like *Buen Vivir*, *Ubuntu* challenges liberal individualism and instrumental rationality. It offers instead a conception of the good life centred on harmony, solidarity, and restorative justice (Nabudere, 2005).

Such framings of development or more precisely alternatives to development as modernity no doubt add indigenous understandings to any discussion of the framing of development. However, what is required to attain or get closer to 'good change' is less certain.

In sum, determining a Global South (GS) perspective on the framing of development is not surprisingly, challenging or in fact impossible. NDPs often, though not always, reflect an elite-driven, state-centric view, which overwhelmingly prioritises material and 'big-D' development by definition (in the sense that they are *national development* plans). In contrast, participatory research offers a different lens, capturing both material and non-material dimensions of development, including social exclusion, power dynamics, and broader wellbeing. Large-scale participatory studies are rare, and the most recent was in the late 1990s. It is difficult to assess whether these perspectives have changed over time, especially as the available data pre-date substantial income increases across much of the GS. Indigenous understandings, such as *Buen Vivir* and *Ubuntu*, add a further layer to the framing of development. As with NDPs and participatory assessments, their representativeness is difficult to assess in terms of broad-based support. And their practical consequences too are open to question. Given the inherent difficulty of identifying a GS perspective on framing of development, it is worth looking at the empirical record of development. This will at least allow for a determination of whether development to date has been transformational or more modest in scope in practice. An important caveat: This method is inherently materialist, nevertheless, it provides basis to evaluate development and the extent of transformation and, also for understanding the critiques of development to date. The next section thus turns to this empirical record to assess development outcomes in the GS.

3.4 Development and Transformation to Date

This section examines the empirical record of development to assess whether it has been transformational in any sense or whether its impact has been more modest. The extent of transformation depends on perspective and measurement. On the one hand, there is evidence that some countries have experienced significant rising average incomes and poverty reduction. On the other hand, development has been uneven, with many countries seeing limited transformation, and economic stagnation and relatively few GS countries achieving the kind of structural transformation in any way akin to the advanced nations' historical experiences.

3.4.1 Global Income Inequality

One can ask: what has happened to world and global income inequality? The former is weighted inequality between countries. The latter is inequality between all individuals' incomes across the globe. Over the past few decades, both world and global inequality have declined, suggesting a convergence between countries and people. This would imply a degree of transformational development. However, this decline has been driven primarily by China (and, to a lesser extent, India and other fast-growing Global South economies) (Gradín, 2021; Kanbur et al., 2024). When China is excluded, the trend of decreasing inequality is far less pronounced. If both China and India are removed from the data, the trend disappears entirely in recent years (see Figures 3.1 and 3.2). This suggests that development has been highly concentrated, with transformational growth occurring in some GS countries. Many

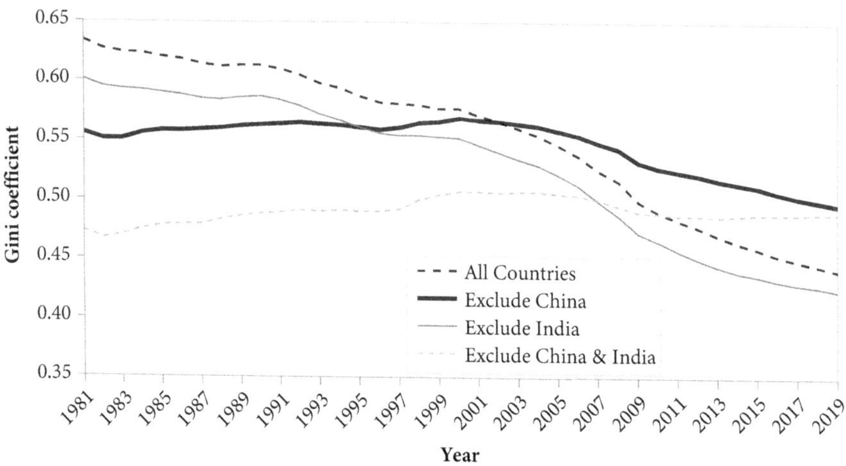

Figure 3.1 World income inequality (population weighted), with and without China and India, 1981–2019
Source: Data from Kanbur et al. (2024).

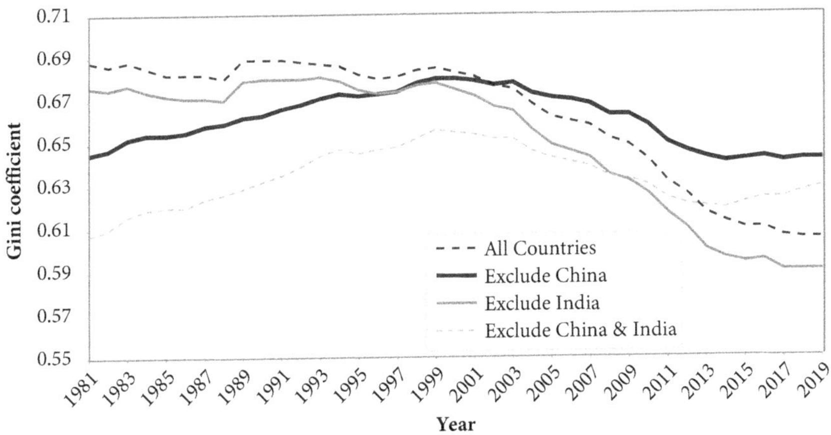

Figure 3.2 Global income inequality, with and without China and India, 1981–2019
Source: Data from Kanbur et al. (2024).

others have experienced more modest change relative to GN countries, and the pattern of catch-up is uneven (see Chapter 4).

Moreover, the era of China-driven world and global inequality reduction is likely over. As China moves closer to the income levels of high-income countries (HICs), and pulls away from other GS countries, it will potentially reverse the decline in world and global inequality. This is a trend Kanbur et al. (2024) refer to as a 'global inequality boomerang'. Even if middle-income countries (MICs) continue to grow, their increasing divergence from LICs could increase global inequality overall in future years. Additionally, while historically, manufacturing employment is associated with rising prosperity (Baymul and Sen, 2020), many MICs are now experiencing 'premature deindustrialization' (Rodrik, 2016). This means a shift away from manufacturing before achieving industrialisation akin to what the advanced nations achieved. Many of the world's poorest countries face weak growth prospects, making large-scale transformation less likely in the future (IMF, 2025).

3.4.2 Rising Incomes alongside Persistent Poverty and Precarity

Another measure of transformation is absolute income growth in GS countries (as opposed to the relative income growth or 'catch up' in the previous discussion). Across much of the GS, per capita income has increased over time, suggesting broad economic progress. The number of low-income countries has declined dramatically. Many LICs have moved into the 'middle-income' category, as classified by the World Bank. This is defined at the low line of about $1000 GNI per year in what is an adjusted market exchange rate conversion. At the same time, extreme poverty (defined as living under $2.15 per day, in 2017 PPP$) has declined. However, these figures mask the continued prevalence of economic insecurity. While some countries have seen sustained growth, poverty and precarity remain widespread, and the benefits of rising incomes have not been evenly distributed.

Whilst overall extreme poverty has fallen, not only is this largely driven by China and India, but poverty measures can also be misleading. Since the 1990s, monetary extreme poverty has unambiguously declined as a share of the total global population. However, extreme monetary poverty may be inadequate for portraying the multidimensional nature of poverty. If we consider poverty across LICs and MICs, the correlation between monetary and non-monetary headcounts is much stronger at the World Bank's $3.65 'moderate' poverty line. It is weaker at the $2.15 line (see Sumner and Yusuf, 2024a, 2024b). Further, although extreme monetary poverty has declined as a share of the global population since the 1990s (see Figure 3.3), it remains very high in certain regions (e.g., sub-Saharan Africa). And, although some GS countries report low levels of extreme poverty, rates of child stunting remain alarmingly high. In parts

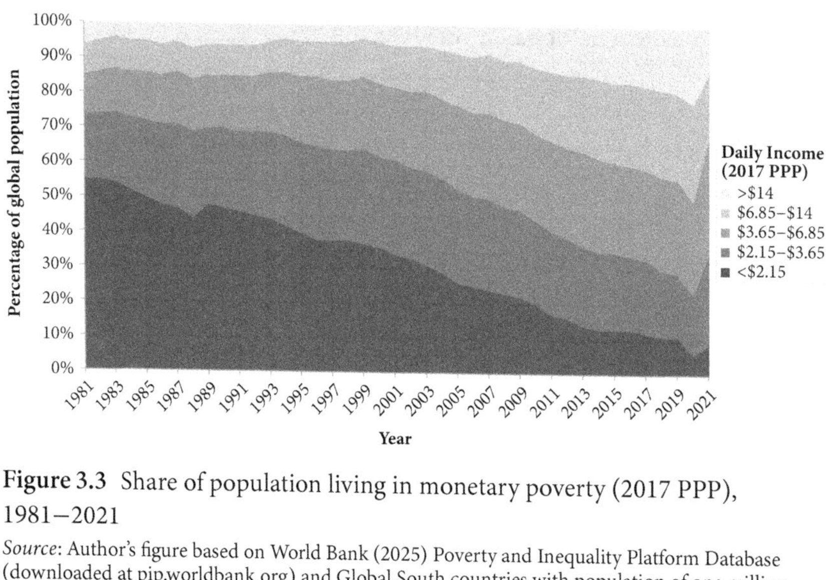

Figure 3.3 Share of population living in monetary poverty (2017 PPP), 1981–2021

Source: Author's figure based on World Bank (2025) Poverty and Inequality Platform Database (downloaded at pip.worldbank.org) and Global South countries with population of one million or more. Regional averages used for missing data.

of Southeast Asia, as many as one in four or even one in three children under five are stunted in the same countries despite extreme monetary poverty at low levels (Sumner and Yusuf, 2024a, 2024b). This is particularly alarming as stunting in childhood has long-run impacts on physical and cognitive development. This suggests that development to date, as measured by typical performance indicators, may not have been so transformational in many countries. This in particular underscores the limits of average income-based measures of transformation as economic progress has not necessarily translated into improved wellbeing across all dimensions of people's lives.

Moreover, escaping poverty does not guarantee security from future poverty. Many people move in and out of poverty, with small economic shocks, such as job loss, illness, or climate-related disasters, pushing millions back below the poverty line (as happened during the COVID pandemic) (Sumner et al., 2022). This fragility highlights the precarious nature of development gains. In fact, global poverty estimates themselves are ultra-sensitive to the chosen poverty threshold, for every 20-cent increase in the extreme poverty line ($2.15), an additional 150 million people would be added to the poverty headcount (see Figure 3.4). And a further one billion people live not far above the extreme poverty line but still in 'absolute' poverty, i.e., under

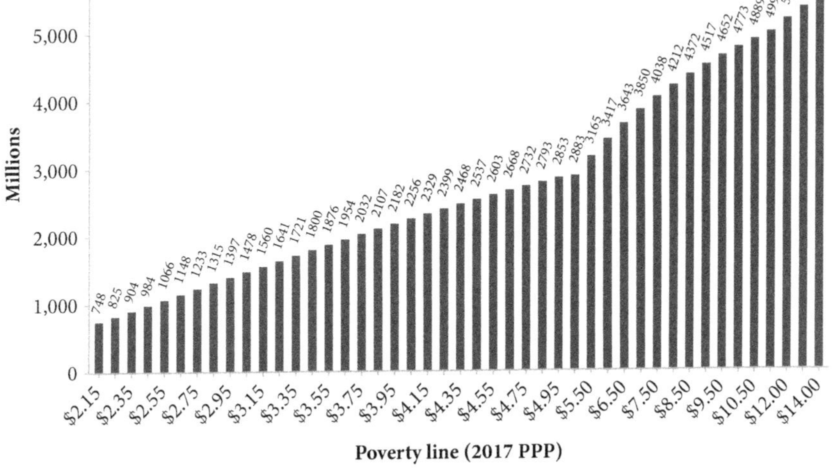

Figure 3.4 Global monetary poverty headcount, 2022 (2017 PPP)

Source: Author's figure based on World Bank (2025) Poverty and Inequality Platform Database (downloaded at pip.worldbank.org) and Global South countries with population of one million or more. Regional population-weighted averages were used to fill in missing data.

the $3.65 line. Poverty rises to over five billion people when using the highest, $14 per person per day, poverty line. Longitudinal studies associate this level with a low risk of falling back into absolute poverty (López-Calva and Ortiz-Juárez, 2014; World Bank, 2023) (see also Figure 3.3). This would suggest that development has been fundamentally transformational for only a relatively small percentage of the global population who will have reached security from future poverty (see Figure 3.4).

The implications of this are profound: while development has lifted some out of extreme poverty, it has not provided lasting economic security for a substantial share of the GS population. On the other hand, there has been substantial structural transformation and mean income growth in a number of MICs though that too has stalled (see later discussion).

3.4.3 The Declining Role of Foreign Aid

A more fundamental shift in development has been the declining role of foreign aid (ODA) in most GS countries. In many countries, aid now plays a smaller role. Sustained growth means many GS countries no longer rely on traditional aid flows (see Figures 3.5 and 3.6 and discussion below). In terms of the net ODA received as a share of GNI threshold (the most commonly available data series), the median is close to 2% of ODA/GNI. OECD (2003) defined high aid dependency as net ODA received as a share of GNI greater than 9%. In the 2022 data, only fourteen countries have a ratio above 9%.[2] For most GS countries, aid plays a small role. Instead, domestic resources and alternative financial flows (such as private foreign borrowing, foreign direct investment, remittances, and government bonds) have become the financiers of development. There is thus a bifurcation between GS countries where aid is important and many GS countries where traditional aid has become largely irrelevant because of the growth of domestic state resources. These post-ODA countries also counter-intuitively are home to about two-thirds of absolute poverty worldwide (Sumner and Yusuf, 2024a, 2024b). The bifurcation within the GS demonstrates a change materially for much of the GS. While aid remains crucial in certain contexts, it is far less dominant than in the past in much of the GS.

[2] Data based on World Bank (2025) and 113 countries with population above one million people. In all figures, median is calculated on entire dataset (outliers are only removed from plots).

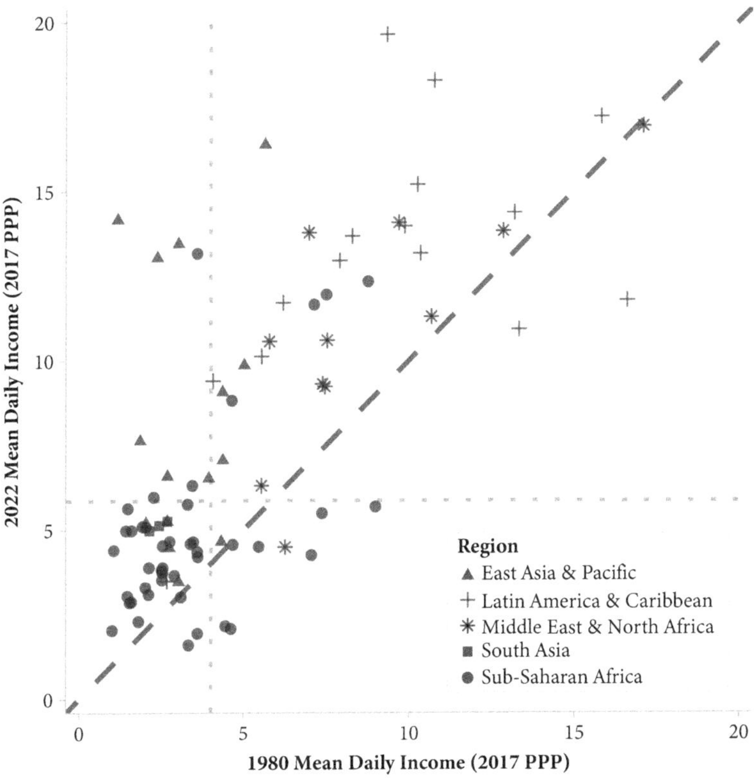

Figure 3.5 Mean daily income per capita (2017 PPP) in countries of the Global South, 1980 and 2022 (or nearest years available)

Source: Author's figure based on World Bank (2025) Poverty and Inequality Platform Database (downloaded at pip.worldbank.org) and Global South countries with population of one million or more.

Note: Countries with no data for 1980 or countries that did not exist in 1980, 1990, or early 1990s data are used. Outliers included in median but not plotted: Brazil (8.4, 21.0); Lebanon (7.5, 30.8); Costa Rica (5.9, 22.2); Argentina (35.2, 22.8); and Malaysia (13.2, 29.4).

Many post-ODA countries have experienced some industrialisation, though this process has stalled in recent years (see Figure 3.8). In the 1970s/1980s/1990s, East Asian countries successfully pursued manufacturing-led employment pathways. By contrast, most contemporary shifts in Global South countries are experiencing shifts either directly from agriculture to low-productivity informal urban services, or from manufacturing employment into services (Baymul and Sen, 2020). This shift to services hinders GS countries' development prospects given that it is typically associated with lower income levels than widespread manufacturing employment. Thus, while development has been transformational in many post-ODA GS countries in

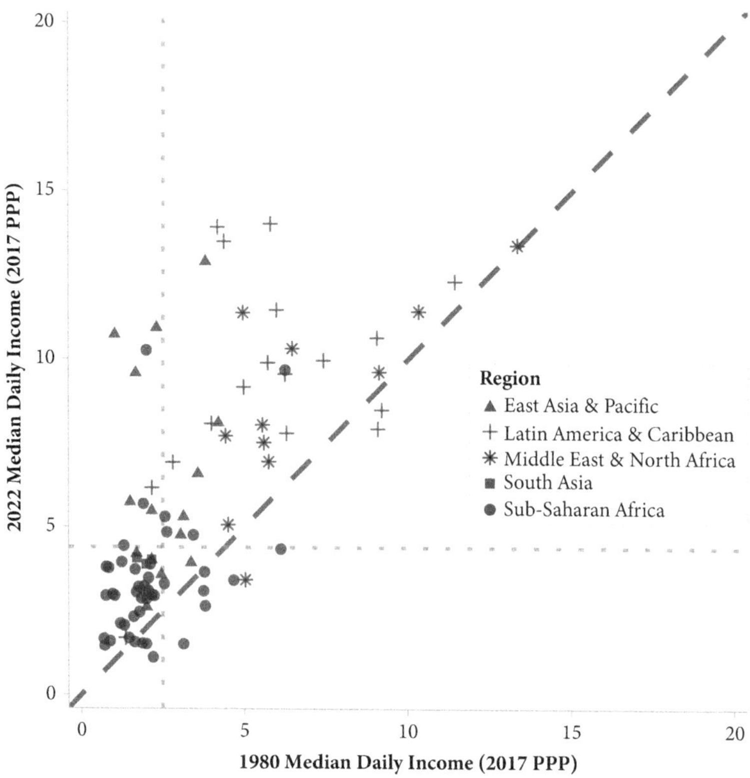

Figure 3.6 Median daily income per capita (2017 PPP) in countries of the Global South, 1980 and 2022 (or nearest years available)

Source: Author's figure based on World Bank (2025) Poverty and Inequality Platform Database (downloaded at pip.worldbank.org) and Global South countries with population of one million or more.

Note: Countries with no data for 1980 or countries that did not exist in 1980, 1990, or early 1990s data are used. Outliers included in median but not plotted: Lebanon (5.6, 26.1); Argentina (25.4, 17.2); and Malaysia (8.5, 21.6).

terms of reducing aid dependency, it has not necessarily been transformative in terms of creating economic structure similar to advanced nations.

If we take a closer look at the data, we can see what did or did not change in absolute terms. Figures 3.5 and 3.6 show the mean and median daily income per capita (in 2017 purchasing power parity) for countries in the Global South in 1980 and in 2022 (or nearest available years). The data here comes from household surveys, since mean income from national accounts may exaggerate household income. Moreover, changes in national accounts do not always flow through fully to households. Most GS countries are above the 45-degree line. This indicates higher income in 2022 than in 1980. In some cases, substantial

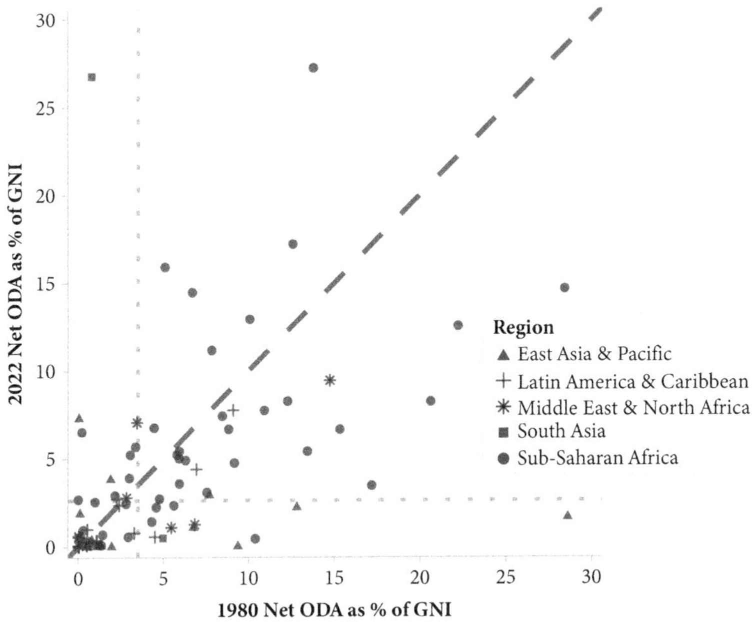

Figure 3.7 Net ODA received as a percentage of GNI in countries of the Global South, 1980 and 2022 (or nearest years available)

Source: Author's figure based on World Bank (2025) database (downloaded at https://data360.worldbank.org/) and Global South countries with population of one million or more.

Note: Countries with no data for 1980 or countries that did not exist in 1980, 1990, or early 1990s data are used. Outliers included in median but not plotted: Syrian Arab Republic (15.1, 36.3); Yemen (3.6, 38.0); Somalia (79.7, 19.1); Cambodia (46.3, 4.0); and Jordan (40.0, 4.1).

so. Though overall, both the mean and median income across the GS have not risen substantially (see median lines on Figures 3.5 and 3.6).

Figure 3.7 depicts the net official development assistance (ODA) received as a percentage of gross national income (GNI) in countries of the Global South, comparing 1980 and 2022 (or nearest available years). The data indicates that the level of net ODA received as a percentage of GNI has generally decreased over this time period across the GS. Most of the plots are under the 45-degree line. Points below the line indicate lower ODA/GNI in 2022 than in 1980, suggesting a shift in the reliance on aid for development in the GS. A subset remains above the line, indicating rising aid dependence among countries that appear 'stuck'. That said, the median for the sample has fallen.

What about economic development? Figure 3.8 presents data on manufacturing value added as a percentage of GDP in countries of the Global South, comparing 1980 and 2022 (or nearest available years). The data shows as many

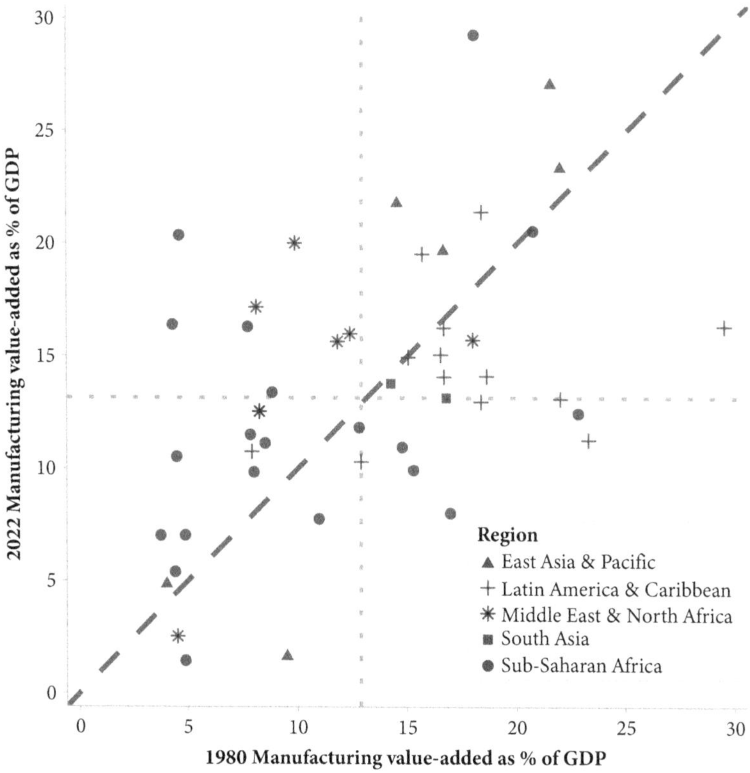

Figure 3.8 Manufacturing value-added as a share of GDP in countries of the Global South, 1980 and 2022 (or nearest years available)

Source: Author's figure based on GGDC 10-Sector and UNUWIDER ETD datasets, and Global South countries with population of one million or more.

Note: Countries with no data for 1980 or countries that did not exist in 1980, 1990, or early 1990s data are used. Outliers included in median but not plotted: China (32.0, 27.1); Mongolia (32.7, 7.1); and Algeria (34.5, 10.2).

countries above the 45-degree line as below it. This means Global South countries are equally split between rising and falling manufacturing value-added shares over time. The median is roughly 13% in both 1980 and 2022. It barely changed. To put this into historical context, the OECD countries typically reached about 25% and East Asia over 30%. In short, GS countries' median remains far below the historic peak of industrialisation in the GN.

In sum, the data is consistent with widespread rising mean and median incomes across much of the GS and declining aid dependency. However, as many Global South countries have increased their manufacturing shares as those where shares have declined. The median in 2022 is about the same as four decades earlier. It remains far below the peak manufacturing shares of value-added historically achieved in OECD countries or East Asia. Consequently, most of the GS still does not have the structural characteristics of the economies of the GN (See discussion in depth on this in Chapter 4).

3.4.4 The Limits of Growth

There are several reasons why development has not been more transformative to date in the ODA-dependent GS. A larger question is why transformation has not been more substantial in the post-ODA GS. The empirical shift towards rising incomes in the GS has undoubtedly improved the economic wellbeing overall. However, it is essential to recognise the paradox of persistent absolute poverty. This paradox can be attributed to a variety of factors such as income inequality, regional disparities, and the unequal distribution of growth within countries (see discussion in Sumner, 2016). In short, the paradox illustrates the limits of economic growth as a sole indicator.

On average, the poverty headcount falls and the incomes of the poor rise in line with economic growth (see Dollar and Kraay, 2002; Dollar et al., 2013; Kraay, 2006). However, some recent contributions have illustrated that this is not always the case: During 'immiserising' growth episodes, average incomes rise but the incomes of the poor or the poorest do not (See Kanbur and Shaffer, 2019; Shaffer, 2024). Shaffer (2023), using the World Bank's Poverty and Inequality Platform data, notes that in a number of growth episodes (meaning rising average incomes for at least five years, based on data from 1990 to 2023), poverty does not fall and/or the incomes of the poorest do not rise. These 'anti-poor' episodes of growth are particularly evident in sub-Saharan Africa (SSA) and Latin America and even evident in East Asia to a lesser extent. However, such episodes are not evident in Europe nor South Asia (see Table 3.1).

Consequently, it appears that the transformational potential of economic growth can be particularly limited in SSA and Latin America. The reason is that SSA and Latin America, in general, have high levels of income inequality and the poorest have low shares of income. Thus, the poorest benefit less from increases in average income and sometimes not at all. Taking a micro-lens, this could reflect that there is a minimum level of assets required to accumulate more assets and raise income (i.e., minimum land or herd sizes or cash advances to buy farming inputs). Alternatively, it could be that conflict may lead to loss of assets, reduced production, and insecurity for the poorest, even amid overall economic growth. Alternatively, it could be that stressors or shocks, droughts, floods, harvest failures, among the poorest are so substantial

Table 3.1 Economic growth episodes and income evolution among the poorest 10% and 20% of population, by region (five-year spells), 1990–2023

	Poorest 10%			Poorest 20%		
	# of episodes without income rise	Total # of episodes	% of episodes without income rise	# of episodes without income rise	Total # of episodes	% of episodes without income rise
East Asia and Pacific	4	23	17.4	3	30	10.0
Europe and Central Asia	0	9	0.0	0	13	0.0
Latin America	11	53	20.8	9	56	16.1
Middle East and North Africa	1	7	14.3	3	16	18.8
South Asia	0	13	0.0	0	14	0.0
Sub-Saharan Africa	12	50	24.0	12	53	22.6
Total	**28**	**155**	**18.1**	**27**	**182**	**14.8**

Note: Growth episodes are defined as episodes of rising average incomes for at least five years.

Source: Shaffer (2023) based on the World Bank's (2024) Poverty and Inequality Platform (PIP) dataset.

that they negate attempts at progress. However, there is a story highlighting the limits of transformational development that is a much broader, adopting more of a macro-view, and that is the shift in the model of development in terms of the global economy.

3.4.5 The Reconfiguration of the Global Economy

A broader view shows that the economic transformation that began in the GS has not been sustained due to changes in the global economy. Further, the meaning of transformation itself has been diminished. Economic transformation in the 1960s meant that countries were developing national productive capacities across all sectors. In other words, substantial and sustained structural transformation, as per Seers' (1963) codification of the characteristics of advanced nations. However, since the 1990s, the rise of global value chains (GVCs) has reshaped the global economy. After the conclusion of the Cold War, the economies of the GS experienced rapid liberalisation, which was promoted by the International Monetary Fund and the World Bank amid the sense of capitalism's triumph at the end of the Cold War. This liberalisation, combined with technological and transportation advancements, enabled the restructuring of global production. As a result, transnational corporations were able to distribute the production of a single final product across numerous countries and locate production based on cost and logistics, thereby creating a 'global value chain world'. Rather than pursuing broad-based national industrialisation, many GS countries have been integrated into global production networks, often as low-value-added suppliers (Phillips, 2017). This has weakened the link between economic transformation and national development.

Engagement in GVCs has also often reinforced income inequality within developing countries. The bargaining power of labour has weakened, and wage shares have declined (World Bank, 2020). The introduction of labour-saving technologies has further displaced low-skilled workers, exacerbating economic inequality (Timmer et al., 2014). Consequently, while GVCs have created opportunities for participation, they have not necessarily delivered deep, long-term transformation for most GS economies. Higher-value activities, such as research and development, design, distribution, and advertising, tend to be situated at the commencement and conclusion of production and are less likely to be situated in the GS. Much of the activity in the GS relates, at best, to lower-value-adding assembly tasks, such as manufacturing, assembly, and retail/sales, in the middle of GVCs. Therefore, GVC participation may bring a shallow mode of industrialisation through some growth in productivity, jobs, and exports, but long-term or deep economic development may be impeded because entire industries are not developed. Further, the advantages of GVC participation may be non-linear and may initially accrue but then diminish or even become negative for employment or value-added in the long term (See Pahl and Timmer, 2020). This may explain the emergence of early deindustrialisation in the GS.

3.4.6 Deindustrialisation in the GS

Many MICs in the GS face not a process of industrialisation but one of deindustrialisation, certainly of employment, and some too of value-added and some of both (Palma, 2006; Rodrik, 2016; Sumner, 2022). This has three major implications. Deindustrialisation is happening at lower levels of per capita income and at smaller manufacturing shares of value-added and employment. The potential economic and social benefits of manufacturing may not be fully realised. Second, MICs are less prepared to cope with the consequences of deindustrialisation because of their weaker welfare regime mechanisms, such as unemployment benefits and access to retraining programs, which cover a smaller share of the population than advanced economies. Third, as noted, contemporary deindustrialisation is taking place in a highly fragmented global production landscape characterised by GVCs. And MICs are unlikely able to shift their focus towards higher-value service activities or upstream activities linked to science and technology as a response to deindustrialisation. This is because these areas have already been captured by countries in the Global North. MICs compete with GN countries like France and Germany as well as China, which subsidise activities to either maintain or capture higher value-added entry points.

In sum, despite economic growth, reductions in extreme poverty, and declining aid dependence, development has not been transformational in a broader sense. Many post-ODA GS countries face an early deindustrialisation. For transformation to be meaningful, economic development must be reclaimed as national development, with a focus on structural transformation, domestic industrial capacity, and broad-based productivity gains. Historically, industrialisation has been the most successful pathway to rapid and sustained economic growth. A thriving manufacturing sector creates backward and forward linkages, drives innovation, expands employment, and generates government revenue, all of which contribute to inclusive and lasting development.

Reclaiming national economic development is important. Why? First, national development in the form of manufacturing expansion in developing countries is key to reducing both components of global inequality: within- and between-country inequality. The expansion of manufacturing value-added fuels faster economic growth and hence has the power to reduce between-country inequality. Empirical support is abundant showing that countries that have raised income dramatically have done so through the process of industrialisation (see Sumner, 2022). At the same time, manufacturing also has more potential than any other sector to expand wage employment opportunities and thus decrease within-country inequality. Of course, any process of industrialisation needs energy and materials. Obtaining and using both necessarily implies increasing greenhouse gas emissions and increasing resource extraction in the Global South. The case can be made it is for the North to reduce energy and material use per capita in order that GS countries have the option to raise these from much lower levels than evident in the GN. Second, as manufacturing industries grow and diversify, they create demand for various goods and services, stimulating investment and consumption across multiple sectors of the economy. This multiplier effect not only fuels further economic expansion but also fosters a more inclusive growth trajectory by creating opportunities for small and medium enterprises and informal sector workers. Economic development, as defined by the shift in productive structure, initiates a virtuous cycle of development by expanding employment and thus domestic demand. Finally, economic development has substantial fiscal implications, enabling funding social welfare provision and public goods investments, as well as infrastructure such as transportation networks, energy systems, and communication facilities. As economies transition towards higher productivity sectors, they generate increased tax revenues, which can be channelled towards funding welfare regimes and public services.

3.5 Conclusion

This chapter has examined competing framings of development, the empirical record, and the reasons why development has not been more transformational in the GS. Development can be understood as both a material process and outcome or as a discourse (albeit with material world consequences) and intentional (willed) and unintentional (unwilled) aspects. This chapter argued for reclaiming the idea of 'big-D' or willed development, which is often dismissed as normatively problematic, top-down, and aid-industry driven. The concept of intentional development requires recasting from an emancipatory perspective. Rather than viewing willed development as an external imposition, it can be reclaimed in the spirit of the Bandung Conference, independence movements, and the aspirations of GS leaders in the 1950s and 1960s.

The discussion then turned to the empirical record of transformative development. While development has been transformational in many GS countries, this transformation has been partial. The GS has also bifurcated into post-ODA and highly ODA-dependent countries, reflecting differing trajectories. The chapter also explored why development has not been more transformational. In ODA-dependent GS countries, transformation is still in its early stages, while in post-ODA countries, economic development has stalled. Instead of industrialising, many LICs in the GS have transitioned from agriculture to informal services employment, which are characterised by lower productivity, lower wages, and fewer opportunities for upward mobility. Whilst post-ODA GS countries, typically MICs, face a process of deindustrialisation and associated consequences.

Finally, this chapter made a case, albeit with caveats, for defining development as the socio-economic transformation of society by national economic development. While rising incomes have led to incremental improvements in wellbeing, they have not fundamentally altered the productive structures of GS economies or improved life chances in the way that structural transformation did for the Global North. In this sense, socio-economic transformation in the form of national economic development represents an emancipatory vision of development.

4
Continuum II
The Scope of Development

Development and its Discontents. Andy Sumner, Oxford University Press. © Andy Sumner (2026).
DOI: 10.1093/9780198902904.003.0004

4.1 Introduction

In this chapter, we turn to the scope of development and discuss whether development is universal, meaning occurring across *all* countries, regardless of whether they are in the Global South (GS) or the Global North (GN). In short, are all countries developing? Are all countries facing similar developmental problems? Are there 'common challenges'? If so, this would imply that Development Studies should take a universalistic position on the continua of the scope of development. If not, then Development Studies should remain centred on the GS.

The chapter thus whether the Brandt Commission's 'line' (see the Independent Commission on International Development Issues, 1980) dividing the globe, or Seers' (1963) 'special case' argument that the advanced countries are different, still stand forty-five to sixty years later. In other words, are GN and GS still fundamentally different in terms of characteristics and how they are positioned in the world? Or is the binary so blurred that it is meaningless. In this chapter, we ask what the case is for universalist positions on the study of development or alternatively, what the salience is of continuing to distinguish between the GS and GN.

Over the last decade or so, proponents of what has become labelled 'global development' (studies) have criticised the salience of binaries evident in the labels of the Global North and the Global South and called for Development Studies to focus on all countries rather than just the Global South (e.g., Horner and Hulme, 2019a; Leach et al., 2021; 2024). They argue that common challenges, such as climate change and inequality, which transcend geographic or economic boundaries, highlight the need for a more universalist focus. In contrast, other scholars (Fischer, 2019; 2019;. Wiegratz et al., 2023) have questioned such calls and have argued that there is a continued relevance of the Global South focus of Development Studies as an expression of fundamental asymmetries in global income, wealth, and power. They point to the persistent subordinate position of the Global South in the global political economy.

The overall argument of the chapter is to concur with the latter in that to dispense with the differentiation between GS and GN risks losing sight of the key structural constraints to any kind of development for the GS. Further, although there has been substantial economic growth across much of the GS, global inequality persists along the lines of history. The divide between colonisers and colonised remains because there has been much less substantial convergence in the structural characteristics of GS with GN countries. As noted in previous chapters, over the past fifty or so years, only a limited number of GS nations, primarily in East Asia, have achieved sustained industrialisation and reduced income per capita disparities with industrialised countries (Wade, 2018).

Some developmental issues may indeed be common in source (e.g., climate change) but manifest in different way in the GS compared to the GN, making the 'common' aspect of limited meaning. In other words, the exposure to, and ability to respond to, the 'common challenge' is different. Further, other developmental issues (e.g., widespread absolute poverty) are highly specific to the GS. Or they are of such a different qualitative or quantitative nature in the GS compared to the GN that it is meaningless to say that they are common across the GN and GS. Moreover, the capacity to respond to any issue in terms of financial resources, state capacity, or human capital are quite different in the GS relative to the GN even in post-ODA GS.

Instead of saying that the binary is blurred, this chapter argues that there is a trinary (re)emerging, somewhat akin to the 'First/Second/Third World' or 'core/semi-periphery/periphery' (including here Wallerstein's term for countries 'in-between' the core and the periphery, see Wallerstein, 1974b; 1976). Specifically, there are the GN countries with their own policy problems such as stagnating economies though in principle with the resources and capacities to deal with these. Then, there are the post-ODA GS countries that have experienced substantial economic growth and rising average income, where official development assistance (ODA) no longer matters. However, emancipation from ODA co-exists with persistent subordination in the global economy through for example, higher borrowing costs for GS countries than GN countries; balance of payment constraints; and that most global markets are oligopolistic and dominated by Western TNCs. Finally, there are the ODA-dependent GS countries that have experienced little or no economic growth and stagnating incomes that are dependent on ODA for the reasonable functioning of government and public services.

To support the overall trinary argument, the chapter posits that the GS, and even the post-ODA GS, remains different to the GN. Even the post-ODA GS has few of the structural characteristics Seers identified with the special case of the GN, making any discussion about income convergence questionable. There are 'common' sources of problems but uncommon manifestations of problems, and highly differentiated abilities to respond even in the post-ODA GS, let alone the ODA-dependent GS. The power and the control of the prospects for future development, in terms of who holds power in the global economy, continue to remain with the GN and to some extent China. Thus, this chapter argues for retaining a demarcation between GN and GS, albeit with an update to consider the bifurcation of the GS and thus the re-emergence of a trinary.

The chapter is structured as follows. Section 2 discusses differentiation within the GS and convergence/divergence between the GS and the GN. Section 3 then turns to the universality argument of 'common' problems. Section 4 focuses on the issue of persisting power of the GN over the GS in the global economy and the GN's control of prospects for development in the GS. Section 5 concludes.

4.2 Binaries, Convergence, Divergence, and the Special Case

4.2.1 Binaries and Trinaries

Since its establishment, DS has been generally concerned with analysing socio-economic development in what are usually labelled 'developing countries' or the 'Global South'. These are typically defined as non-Western or non-advanced countries. Of course, much of that research does not ignore the Global North. Indeed, the dominance of the GN's transnational corporations or the GN's dominance in decision-making at the board of the International Monetary Fund (IMF) and the World Bank for example should be part of DS as well as the policies of those GN-dominated institutions. However, the countries of the GN in and of themselves are rarely the direct and only focus of DS.

The original binary of DS, meaning categorisations of nations as developing/developed or Global South/Global North, has long been critiqued by scholars working within and outside DS for failing to represent complex reality (Haug, 2021; Haug et al., 2021; Sud and Sanchez-Ancochea, 2022). Up to the 1960s, 'underdeveloped' country was the common label. Then, in light of the JFK-initiated 'Decade of Development', 'developing countries' became the most often used label. However, the other term evident for much of the post-WWII period was 'The Third World' credited to Sauvy (1952). This was a reference to a revolutionary pamphlet by Abbe Sieyés, a key figure in the French revolution who wrote of 'the third estate', meaning the masses or commoners. 'Third World' thus originated from an analogy of the French revolution and alluded to the divide between nobility, clergy, and commoners. The GS were the commoners. The term 'Third World' was intended to reflect 'exclusion' rather than 'inferiority' (Scheyvens and Storey, 2003, p. 13).

The dominant lens was trinary: there was a First World, Second World, and Third World. And, for many years, during the Cold War, the GS was labelled the 'Third World'. The term was associated with a loose grouping of newly independent countries in the 1950s and the 1960s. It became associated with the 'non-aligned movement'. Relatedly, the term 'Third World' has also been associated with the G77 (Group of 77), which was formed within the United Nations Conference on Trade and Development (UNCTAD) in the 1960s. Many scholars link 'Global South' politically to this coalition.

As is evident, the term 'Third World' is dated by the Cold War and by a time period with a First World (the industrialised countries) and a Second World (the communist block). The end of the Cold War led to the dissolution of these terms, as the Second World of ex-communist countries, in principle, joined the First World though in reality some of the communist countries joined an ambiguous new group of countries or 'transition economies' transitioning to capitalism from communism. The end of the Cold War necessitated the end of this trinary. Its meaning was no longer relevant. It was clear that the ex-communist countries were no longer a 'Second' World given they no longer had a shared political and economic structure that stood in contrast to the capitalist First World. It was not clear then or even now if those ex-communist countries were part of the GS or GN. Many such countries are Upper MICs, not HICs, and many have some shared characteristics with GS countries. Further, 8 ex-communist countries joined the OECD.

After the Cold War, many terms were in use, each with critiques. For example, less developed countries or low-income countries for the poorest countries. The South (not geographically perfect, but used by the 1980 Brandt Commission and the 1990 South Commission), post-colonial societies, 'Non-OECD', or non-OECD HIC countries (countries not members of the Organisation for Economic Cooperation and Development, historically established to represent the interests of industrialised countries of the GN, but now including middle-income countries from Latin America and accession countries in Asia).

The focus of DS has been on countries of the GS, most of which were colonised by the GN. The process of political decolonisation produced many newly independent states in the 1950s and 1960s, particularly across Africa and Asia, in addition to Latin American independence, which had occurred largely in the early 1800s. Although the countries of the GN itself have not been studied directly in much of DS, the power of the GN in the development of the GS is studied to the extent that there is an influence on the GS, albeit the GS is the primary focus. Why? One reason is a wide range of social sciences have a long history of studying the GN and somewhat neglecting the GS, at least until the last decade or so. DS therefore has a raison d'être in the study of the GS. The GS was, and often still is, the set of countries with acute development problems, not the GN. Another way of looking at this is that the defining split, at least when DS emerged, is between ODA donors and ODA recipients. Today, that is less clear as a growing number of Global South countries operate as providers of development assistance, though with smaller absolute budgets for cooperation. Some are donors and at the same time recipients.

In the 1950s/1960s, the countries of the GS were fundamentally different in characteristics to 'developed' countries by any conceivable metric. Examples include income per capita, absolute poverty rates, or production and export structures. This was the case so much so that Seers (1963) coined the term 'highly special case' to refer to the GN. This was to demarcate how the developed countries were fundamentally different in a range of societal characteristics when compared to developing countries. Seers (1963) provided the seminal discussion of the characteristics of 'developed' countries/GN. In particular, their divergence from the characteristics of developing countries/GS. On this basis, he noted the 'special case' of 'a few countries with highly unusual, not to say peculiar, characteristics' (p. 80), meaning those peculiar characteristics of perhaps twenty to thirty countries of the GN at that time that differed dramatically to the more than 100 countries at that time of the GS.

Another dividing line often referred to is the 'Brandt line' of the Brandt Commission (1980). This line is the origin of the North/South demarcation. The line divides the GN and the GS geographically with an underlying economic logic, namely Gross Domestic Product (GDP) per capita. The Brandt line encircles the world around thirty degrees North latitude with deviations and thus includes South, Central, America, Africa, the Middle East, and most of East Asia though with the line lowered to exclude Japan, Australia, and New Zealand (which were defined as part of the GN).

Core and periphery are other terms that differentiate GN and GS. They draw from structuralist and dependency thought. Structuralists made the case for distinguish between 'developing' and 'developed' countries based on the subordinate position of periphery (GS) countries within the global political economy dominated by core (GN) countries. Wallerstein (1976) added 'semi-periphery' countries to identify countries of the periphery that were industrialising, and which had structural characteristics in-between the core and the periphery, and were also mediating linkages between core and periphery nations. The semi-periphery tends to be exploited by the core. It is also an exploiter of the periphery. Wallerstein's (ibid.) original list of semi-peripheric countries included parts of Latin America (e.g., Brazil, Argentina, and Mexico) as well as East Asia (China, India, Indonesia, Malaysia, and South Korea). It also included a number of OECD countries. This list was updated in Wallerstein (1997) with additional countries in East Asia (e.g., Vietnam) and OECD countries from Eastern Europe.

Another term is 'early' and 'late' developing countries, referring to the extent of influence of the global economy on their development. Early developing countries were less influenced by the global economy because fewer countries were industrial at that time. Then, as each country develops, the global economy changes the development trajectories of other countries. Gerschenkron (1962) is credited with coining the term 'late industrialisation' while Hirschman (1968) introduced the term 'late-late industrialisation'. Additionally, many others were using the concept including Furtado, Lewis, Prebisch, and Singer, including those writing in the dependency tradition (for example, Cardoso and Faletto, 1979; dos Santos, 1970; Frank, 1966; 1967; Furtado, 1964). The idea is evident in much early theorising in classical development economics. It is not always explicitly labelled 'late development'. Gerschenkron (1962) argued that the UK was the sole example of 'early' industrialisation, meaning relatively uninfluenced by the global economy. All other countries were 'late' industrialisers. The concept of late development is not only about the timing of industrialisation. The concept is predicated on the sense that late industrialisers face structural constraints, making the process harder for late industrialising countries because early industrialising countries dominate markets with their companies and their financial institutions.

At present, the 'Global South' label has become the commonly used concept. For this reason, it is used in this book. A US political activist and scholar, Oglesby (1969) is sometimes credited with coining the 'Global South' label (adding the 'global'), though the terms' precise origin is contested. There is within the term an emphasis on the notion of solidarity between the poorer countries of the world. However, even GS is not without problems, with contradictory meanings and uses of the term. For some, it is a reference to developing countries and the hierarchy of the global economy. For others, it is the reference to the marginalised people wherever they live, be it in the GS or the GN. Sud and Sanchez-Ancochez (2022) discuss the 'stickiness' of the term, 'the South', noting its use as a geographical territory as well as a representation of domination. They highlight the structure of the global political economy, racial divisions due to colonialism and slavery, and the distribution of power globally. They note that some uses of the term enhance the power differences of the GN over the GS, while others reduce them. In short, the term is not without problems. The term 'New South' too has gained some prominence (for example, Ishmael, 2024; Gabuev and Stuenkel, 2024). It refers to an emerging group of GS countries that have greater political and economic power. The idea seeks to capture a shift in global political economy that may challenge North–South hierarchy. In contrast to the sense of marginalisation inherent in the GS term, the New South concept seeks to recognise the growing agency of parts of the GS due to economic importance. There is a new assertiveness in global governance showing a shift towards a multipolar world. The significance of northern donors' ODA in the GS is declining with a rising importance of South–South cooperation. In short, the 'New South' is more important in shaping global discussion (most notably, the BRICS+ group and the role in the GS in the G20 and G77).

4.2.2 Income Convergence

As previously discussed, growth in income in many countries of the Global South and changing structural characteristics, i.e., industrialisation, in some parts of the GS have coincided with falling global inequality. This has led to a discussion of whether the boundaries between developed/North and developing/South are so blurred they became meaningless. The latter would imply that development has become (or always was) universal to all countries and thus that the countries of the GN should be as much a focus of DS as are the countries of the GS.

Signs of acceptance of this case include the World Bank dropping the term 'developing countries' in 2016 in its widely utilised World Development Indicators database (see Khokhar and Serajuddin, 2015). The World Bank instead defaulted to an average income classification of low-, lower-middle-, and upper-middle-income countries (LICs, LMICs, and UMICs) versus high-income countries (HICs) by Gross National Income (GNI) per capita (Atlas method; an exchange rate-based conversion with adjustment for inflation differentials between a country and a set of HICs). This is essentially the same as 'developing countries' or GS in the sense that LICs, LMICs, and UMICs are identified as the countries of the GS, while HICs are not.

As noted, the term 'Global South' has largely become the default term for what were labelled 'developing countries' (or the 'Third World' prior to the end of the Cold War). Many countries of the GS have experienced substantial economic growth and some have developed some kind of industrial base. Many are facing the spectre of stalled industrialisation or even early deindustrialisation (see discussion in Chapter 3). Additionally, rather than selling primary products for manufactures, it is fair to say that the foreign trade of many post-ODA GS countries consists of selling manufactures or components of manufactures, though often alongside primary or intermediate/processed primary products (Sumner, 2021).

Empirically, we can ask whether the 'Brandt line' dividing GS and GN or the 'special case' demarcating the GN from the GS still exists in any meaningful way. Regarding the former, Lees (2021) considered empirical tests to assess the 'continuity' or 'erosion' of the Brandt line. They find continuity in terms of absolute income differences, aggregate growth rates, and income rankings between the GN, defined as the OECD countries, and the GS, defined as G77 countries. However, some partial erosion is noted, as the variation in non-oil incomes within the GS grew and the relative economic power of the GS (in terms of relative shares of global GDP, at market exchange rates) increased, though this was largely driven by China. In short, a picture emerges that is consistent with a differentiation within the GS.

These findings are consistent with empirical tests of income convergence. Patel et al. (2021) argue that if one takes the 1960–2010s period, GS countries have not grown faster than GN countries, although since 1995, there has been about twenty years of convergence to about the mid-2010s (see also Johnson and Papageorgiou, 2020). Furthermore, actual convergence is so far in the future to beg the question of how to interpret recent trends. The COVID pandemic and its aftermath too raise a big question over any projections. Even prior to COVID-19, the most sophisticated long-run projections err on the side of caution (see, for example, Fouré et al., 2012). China is potentially one exception, as it is likely to cross over the GNI per capita of the World Bank's classification of 'high-income country' status in the late 2020s. Despite thirty years of rapid economic growth and industrialisation, China's GNI per person remains far below the United States in PPP and at market rates. China's GNI per capita remains under one-third of the US in PPP terms and one-sixth at market exchange rates (World Bank, 2025). If India sustained very rapid growth while the US grew steadily, India could reach US GDP per capita (PPP) near 2070. It does not seem plausible that any country would experience such growth rates for such a long period. These projections do demonstrate that the assumptions needed to accept the eventual convergence are implausibly optimistic. Other BRICS+ countries, such as Brazil and South Africa, are not on a convergence pathway, so they will never catch up on current trends with the US. As noted in Chapter 3, although world and global income inequality have been falling, these are largely due to China. In other words, it is true to say world and global inequality has fallen overall. However, when China is removed, the fall in global inequality is more muted, and without China and India, there is no fall, and there is even a slight rise (see Kanbur et al., 2024).

4.2.3 Structural Convergence and the Special Case

What about convergence in the characteristics of GS countries with those of the GN? In this section, Seers' 'special case' argument is revisited. The thesis is that GS/GN remain different in internal and external, (i.e., how the GS sits in the global hierarchy) characteristics, albeit with a split between ODA-dependent and post-ODA GS countries, meaning countries where ODA no longer matters.

Seers (1963) argued that advanced economies have distinct characteristics. He also, in line with Hirschman (1971; 1981), noted that economics was built around industrial economies. The laws were presented as universal although developing economies have quite different characteristics. Seers (1963, p. 80) argued with reference to GN countries that,

> 'it is inherently implausible that a 'general theory', or even propositions of any generality, can be derived from the experiences of a few countries with highly unusual not to say peculiar, characteristics. Teaching which concentrates on this type of economy is somewhat distorted, and the distortion is dangerous if those teaching fail to stress continually that they are dealing with what is a highly special case.'

Further, Seers argued that too little attention is paid to the export sector and the Keynesian role of the state in the Global North. He stressed that developing countries cannot be understood without reference to the global economy. He also noted that in the Global North, the public sector can offset private sector fluctuations, a capacity much harder for developing countries to achieve.

Seers argued that the path of advanced economies cannot be copied as a general model. Seers' (1963, pp. 81–83) quintessential characteristics of the 'special case' of advanced economies included a lengthy list of structural characteristics. For example, the existence of a diverse manufacturing sector that is much larger than either the agriculture or mining sector and an agricultural sector that is wholly commercial, whilst mining is of limited size. Furthermore, foreign trade characteristics such as exports that have a large internal market and are sold to many countries with high price and income elasticities. Moreover, imports consisting largely of primary products with low income elasticity of demand. Additionally, very few households living below the subsistence level, there is a moderately equal distribution of income, and food does not consume the overwhelming majority of household expenditure. The opposite characteristics were those of the then 'Third World'. Seers (1963, p. 77) summed it up thus:

> Viewed from the point of view of either history or geography, it [the advanced nations] is an extremely rare case, and obviously so. There have been only a few such economies for a few decades; even now they cover only quite a small fraction of [hu]mankind.

The 'special case' characteristics set out by Seers endure as definition of an 'advanced' economy. Seers argued that the 'special case' was peculiar and unrepresentative of the world because of the characteristics of the countries of the GS. Is that still the case?

We can assess, with data caveats, the contemporary relevance of Seers' special case empirically though those data caveats are substantial and there are limitations doing any exercise like this with a large sample of GS countries. First, socio-economic data is generally available for a wide group of GS countries only from about 1980 or 1990 as some low- and middle-income countries did not exist prior to 1990. Taking a step back: The point here is not to assess whether the GS changed in terms of income levels (clearly the post-ODA GS has by definition) but the extent of convergence between the GN.

So, what changed and what did not in relative terms, namely relative to the GN defined as OECD HICs? Figures 4.1 to Figure 4.5 seek to answer this question. Figure 4.1 shows the convergence of the mean income per capita of global south countries with median income per capita in OECD HICs using household survey data. Specifically, the ratio of each GS country to OECD HIC income (set as 100.0 in both 1980 and 2022).[1] GS countries plotted above the 45-degree line were closer to the OECD HICs in 2022 than 1980. Conversely, GS countries plotted below the 45-degree line were further from the OECD HIC in 2022 than 1980. What does the figure show? The median of all GS countries in 1980 was 13.1% and this actually fell to 10.8 in 2022. In short, the average fell slightly. What happened? Although some GS grew much closer to the OECD HIC (for example, China), most

[1] Data based on World Bank (2025) and 113 countries with population above one million people. In all figures, median is calculated on entire dataset (outliers are only removed from plots).

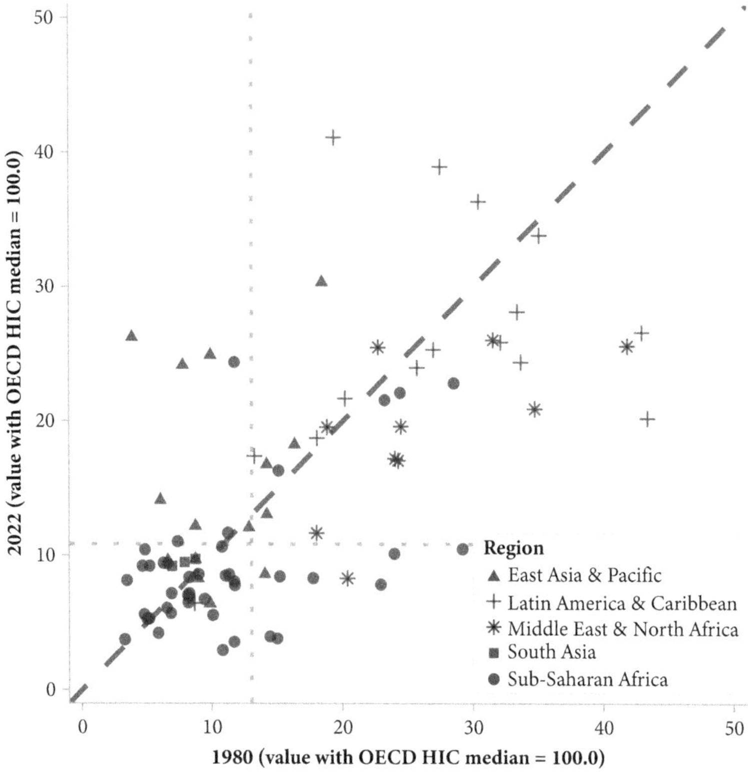

Figure 4.1 Convergence of mean income per capita (2017 PPP) in Global South countries with OECD high-income country (HIC) mean daily income per capita, 1980 and 2022 (or nearest years available)

Source: Author's figure based on World Bank (2025) Poverty and Inequality Platform Database (downloaded at pip.worldbank.org) and Global South countries with population of one million or more.

Note: Countries with no data for 1980 or countries that did not exist in 1980, 1990, or early 1990s data are used. Outliers included in median but not plotted: Venezuela (53.9, 21.8); Lebanon (24.5, 57.0); Jordan (55.5, 31.3); Argentina (114.2, 42.3); Malaysia (43.0, 54.3); and Paraguay (51.4, 31.8).

GS countries either grew on slightly closer (for example, India) or fell back versus the OECD HIC. In short, there has not been widespread convergence of mean income per capita between Global South countries and the OECD high-income countries for 1980 versus 2022. While some GS countries have been closing the gap, the majority continue to lag significantly behind. The overall picture underscores the persistence of income differences between the Global South and OECD HICs.

Mean income comparisons, although typically used for comparisons, may be misleading in the sense that median income is a better reflection of income in a country of the 'average' person. Figure 4.2 shows the convergence of the

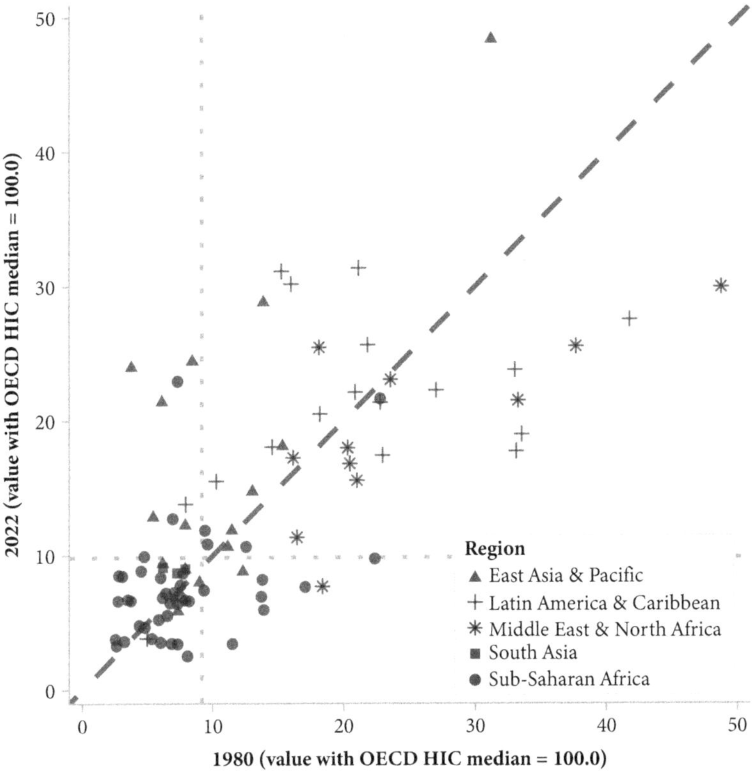

Figure 4.2 Convergence of median income per capita (2017 PPP) in Global South countries with OECD high-income country (HIC) median daily income per capita, 1980 and 2022 (or nearest years available)

Source: Author's figure based on World Bank (2025) Poverty and Inequality Platform Database (downloaded at pip.worldbank.org) and Global South countries with population of one million or more.

Note: Countries with no data for 1980 or countries that did not exist in 1980, 1990, or early 1990s data are used. Outliers included in median but not plotted: Lebanon (20.4, 58.4) and Argentina (92.6, 38.5).

median income per capita of global south countries with median income per capita in OECD HICs using household survey data. Specifically, the ratio of each GS country to OECD HIC income (set as 100.0 in both 1980 and 2022). Again, GS countries plotted above the 45-degree line were closer to the OECD HIC in 2022 than in 1980. Conversely, GS countries plotted below the 45-degree line were further from the OECD HIC in 2022 than 1980. What does the figure show? The cross-country median of GS countries in 1980 was 9.1% and this actually rose marginally to 9.8 in 2022. In short, the median is about the same more than forty years later. Again, although some GS grew

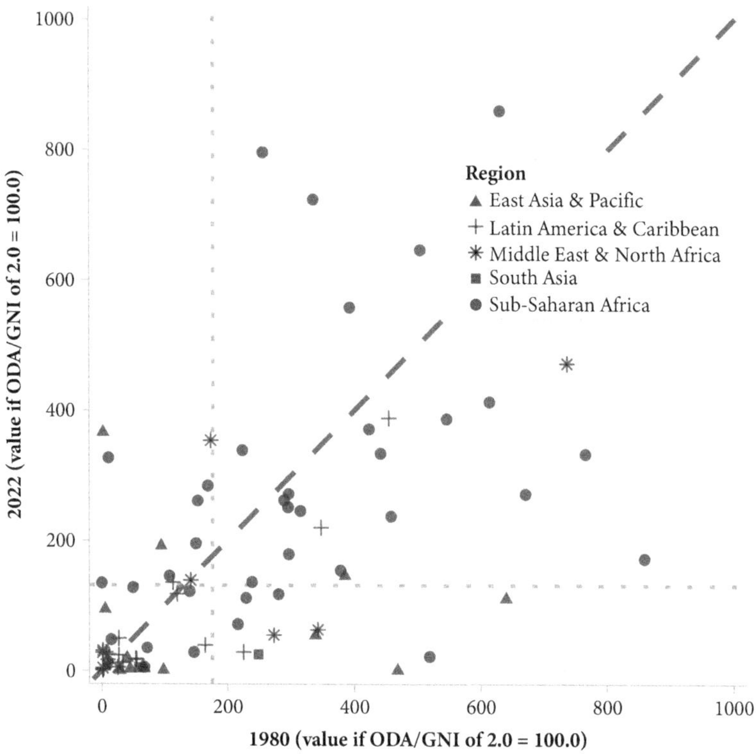

Figure 4.3 Convergence of Global South countries with 'low aid dependency' defined as net ODA received as a % of GNI less than 2%, 1980 and 2022 (or nearest years available)

Source: Author's figure based on World Bank (2025) database (downloaded at https://data360.worldbank.org/) and Global South countries with population of one million or more.

Note: Countries with no data for 1980 or countries that did not exist in 1980, 1990, or early 1990s data are used. Outliers included in median but not plotted.

much closer to the OECD HIC (for example, China), most GS countries either grew slightly (for example, India) or fell back versus the OECD HIC. And those doing better were balanced out by those doing worse. In short, the convergence of median income per capita between Global South countries and the OECD high-income countries is limited. While some countries appear to be closing the gap, the majority continue to lag significantly behind. The slight median rise points to limited convergence as the broader trend. The overall picture again underscores the persistence of income differences between the Global South and OECD HICs. In sum, while a small number of GS countries have seen notable gains, most Global South countries remain far below the OECD HICs.

Figure 4.3 shows the changes in aid dependency in the GS between 1980 and 2022 using the definition of 2% net ODA received as a share of GNI as the 'convergence' with a point of low aid dependency. Specifically, the ODA/GNI ratio of each GS country is plotted indexed to 2.0 in 1980 and 2022. GS countries plotted above the 45-degree line were further from the 2% point in 2022 than 1980. Conversely, GS countries plotted below the 45-degree line were closer to the 2% point in 2022 than in 1980. What does the figure show? The median of all GS countries in 1980 was 175.9 and this fell to 131.2 in 2022. So, what happened? Across the GS, ODA as a share of GNI fell in most of the GS. Looking at Figure 4.3 at the countries where ODA/GNI moved away from the 2.0 point, there are relatively few countries above the 45-degree line substantially. Across the Global South, most cases moved closer to or below the 2% of GNI threshold. That said, a group of countries have worsened markedly.

What about structural transformation? Figure 4.4 depicts the convergence of the manufacturing value-added as a percentage of GDP in the Global South with the OECD HICs. We set the OECD HIC peak as 25.0 based on historic mean and median from advanced nations' peak manufacturing shares in GDP using the period of 1960–2012 for which a comparable dataset is available. Namely, Denmark (24.9, 1974), Spain (22.8, 1988), France (18.6, 1977), UK (26.0, 1974), Italy (27.3, 1995), and Japan (26.2, 1991) (data from the GGDC 10-sector database, 2014 version). Latin American countries generally reached somewhat similar peak manufacturing levels to countries of the GN though many years ago. For example, Mexico (22.4, 2000), Brazil (23.0, 1973), and Chile (23.6, 1972). However, many East Asia countries achieved notably higher peaks. Specifically, South Korea (36.4, 2011), Indonesia (28.4, 2001), Malaysia (29.2, 2000), China (36.5, 2010), and Thailand (37.9, 2010).

This all matters because manufacturing often delivers productivity gains that lift overall growth. Rodrik (2013b) shows that productivity in manufacturing converges unconditionally across countries. This echoes Kaldor's (1966; 1967) first law: that manufacturing growth is the engine of overall economic growth thanks to its dynamic economies of scale and linkages. Historical evidence indicates that no country has achieved high-income status without first undergoing a sustained phase of industrialisation. Szirmai (2012) presents evidence that in late industrialising, countries manufacturing value-added shares peaked at 20%–30% of GDP:

> In [economies] such as [the Republic of] Korea, Taipei, China, and Singapore, the share of manufacturing in GDP increased rapidly to 20–30 per cent, peaking during periods of rapid industrialization before levelling off or declining slightly at high income levels. (p. 20)

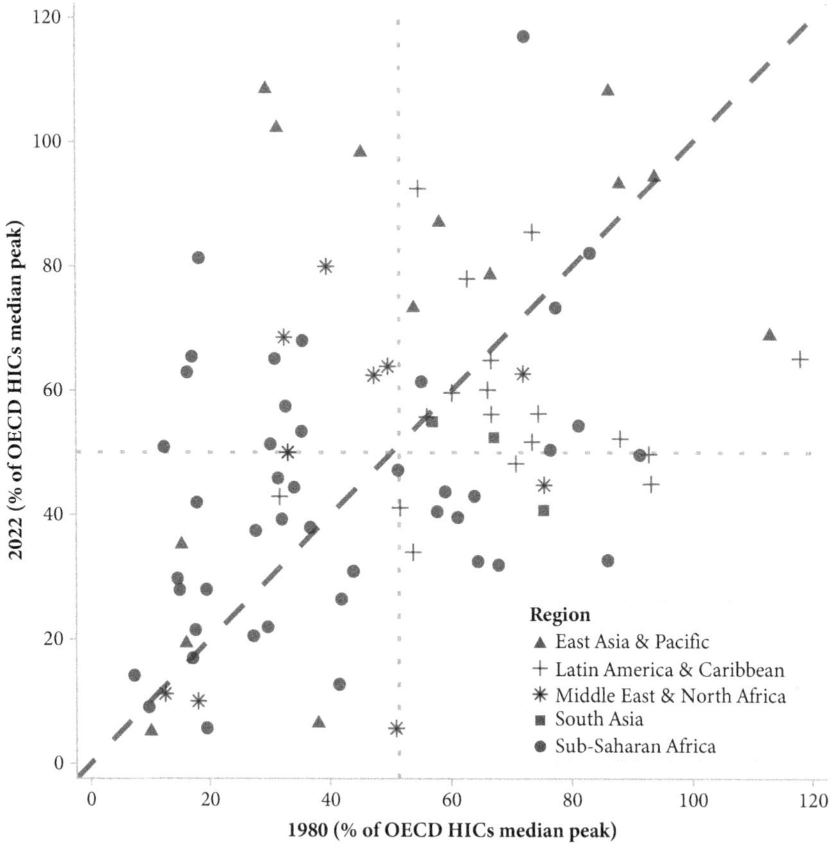

Figure 4.4 Convergence of Global South countries with OECD HIC historical peak of manufacturing share of value-added (median historical peak of OECD = 25.0), 1980 and 2022 (or nearest years available)

Source: Author's figure based on GGDC 10-Sector and UNUWIDER ETD datasets, and Global South countries with population of one million or more.

Note: Countries with no data for 1980 or countries that did not exist in 1980, 1990, or early 1990s data are used. Outliers included in median but not plotted: China (152.0, 108.3); Mongolia (130.8, 28.5); and Algeria (137.9, 40.9).

On the employment side, Felipe et al. (2019) show how economies that successfully transitioned to high-income status typically reached manufacturing employment shares of 18%–20% at their peak:

> All of today's rich non-oil economies enjoyed at least 18% manufacturing employment shares in the past ... [and] many late-industrialising economies are unlikely to meet that 18%–20% employment threshold. (abstract p. 139; pp. 161, 163).

These are not rigid thresholds but empirical regularities observed by studying countries that successfully transitioned to high income. The broader point is that structural transformation, particularly a strong, sustained shift into manufacturing, is historically associated with becoming a rich country and countries that never reach sufficient levels of industrialisation tend to get stuck at middle-income levels or the so-called 'middle-income trap'.[2]

What does Figure 4.4 show? Countries above the 45-degree line are those where the 2022 ratio is higher than 1980, meaning these countries moved closer to the peak or industrialised. Countries below the 45° line are those where the 2022 ratio is lower than 1980. Meaning the countries have moved away from the peak or deindustrialised. The median of all GS countries in 1980 was 51.3 and this fell slightly to 50.1 in 2022. In short, the median level of industrialisation in the GS fell slightly. What happened? More or less equal numbers of GS countries industrialised as deindustrialised.

The above picture is two points in time. If we consider countries in the GS with sufficient data (i.e., about fifty developing countries with high quality data for the period of 1960–2018), we can see that relatively few GS countries achieved 25.0 or more in terms of shares of manufacturing in value-added (see Figure 4.5 below). Only ten of forty-seven GS countries with data reached the OECD-average historic threshold for industrialisation. In other words, two-thirds of GS countries with data have not achieved levels of industrialisation comparable with the OECD countries. Further, in some ways, more important is that many of the peaks are more than twenty years ago. Two-thirds of the GS countries with data had peaks from pre-2000. In fact, many are before the end of the Cold War. Figures 4.4 and 4.5 indicate a split pattern: deindustrialisation in many cases and industrialisation in others. And convergence of Global South countries with the OECD's historical peak manufacturing share in value-added has been limited to about ten GS countries with data. In sum, although many GS countries have had sustained economic growth and rising incomes to some extent and a decline in ODA dependency, talk of convergence is at best many years in the distance. Further, a relatively small number of GS countries that have substantially narrowed the structural characteristics gap in terms of industrialisation in Latin America and in East Asia though, as noted previously, now face a process of deindustrialisation and tertiarisation.

[2] See for a range of discussion on the topic: Doner and Schneider (2016) and in Gill and Kharas (2007). It should be flagged it is not certain if such a trap exists (Kang and Paus 2020) and studies have found there is no generalisable pattern in the form of a 'trap' facing middle-income countries (Pritchett and Summers 2014).

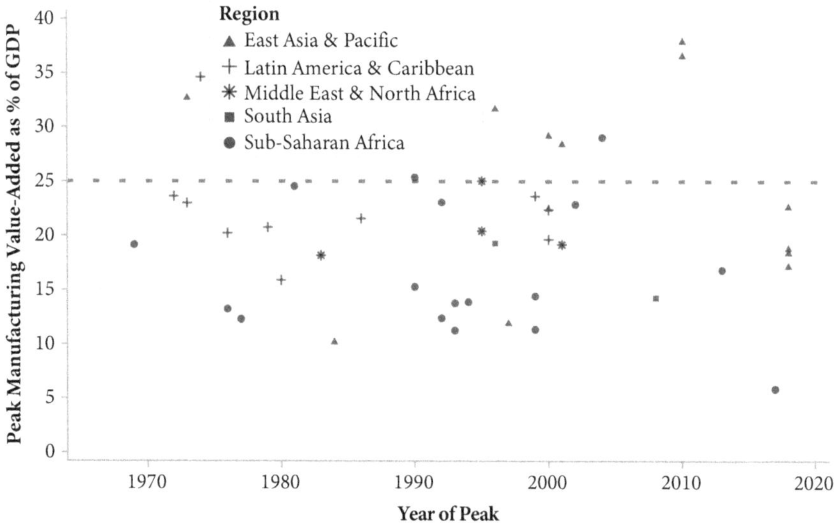

Figure 4.5 Peak manufacturing value-added shares as percentage of GDP in Global South countries and year of peak (horizontal line at 25% = historical median peak of OECD countries).

Source: Author's figure based on GGDC 10-Sector and UNUWIDER ETD datasets, and Global South countries with population of one million or more.

4.3 Universality or Not

4.3.1 Common Problems?

Although many of the preceding points highlight enduring differences between the GN and GS, as noted recent DS scholarship has re-made the case for more universalist framings of development. This discussion revitalises arguments made by Seers (1979) many years ago about bringing Development Studies 'home' to the study of underdevelopment in Europe. The argument for this is two-fold. First, Horner and Hulme (2019a; 2019b) argue that differences between countries of the GN and the GS have blurred sufficiently to make the GN/GS binary of limited meaning in their view. Second, that there are 'common' problems faced across all societies. These oft cited 'common challenges' (referred to by, for example, Leach et al., 2024) are global meta-trends such as climate change that are faced by all countries regardless of whether they are in the GN or GS. There are also 'common' questions in the GN and GS relating to rising living standards, inequalities, employment generation, and public good provision.

The idea of expanding DS to GN analysis has a long history in Development Studies. In the mid-1970s, for a decade or so, Seers, for example, focused his attention on Europe. Seers et al. (1979), set out to move away from what he called European 'paternalism'. In that volume, Seers considered underdevelopment in Europe, arguing that conventional theorising in the social sciences in Europe ignored peripheries and their role in maintaining a core. In short, taking underdevelopment theories usually applied to the then Third World, he sought to explain economic development in the 'core' of Europe defined as the industrial heartlands of France and Germany (and extending to Birmingham, Oslo, Helsinki, and Vienna) and its relationship with underdevelopment of the European 'periphery' (defined in the work as Greece, Southern Italy, Spain, Portugal, Ireland, and the North of England, Wales, Scotland, and Northern Ireland). Seers et al. argued that analysis of underdevelopment in Europe was enriched using Latin American dependency theory, arguing, akin to Latin American dependency theory, that the periphery of Europe was better off being part of the European system connecting it to the European core, but structurally dependent in a hierarchical relationship.

Such thinking of the study of development in the GN has come and gone and returned in DS, fluctuating, and resurfacing from time to time. One example from the late 1990s is Maxwell (1998) who argued that the increase of relative poverty and social exclusion in the North offered an opportunity for dissolving GN/GS boundaries. Maxwell argued that increasing poverty and social exclusion in OECD countries was related to rising inequality, falling political participation, and increasing numbers of a poorly educated and unemployed population, and that these problems are similar in characteristics to those in GS countries. Maxwell further discussed that since the inception of DS in the 1960s, there have been phenomena that brought the North and the South together. For example, deindustrialisation in the North, while there has been urbanisation, economic diversification, a rising manufacturing share of GDP, and increasing literacy in the GS. Further, that key themes in DS that are relevant to both GN and GS, such as poverty reduction and livelihoods, governance, and gender inequality.

If Development Studies were to broaden the scope to 'global' DS (see discussion, Mehta et al., 2006), it would comprise all countries and the interconnectedness of development, poverty, wealth, and wellbeing in North/West and South/East. It would be based on the rationale that 'development' will be (even) more about the interconnectedness of North/West and South/East in the years ahead. Proponents of that note the COVID pandemic, as well as the 2007/2008 global financial crisis, demonstrated the extent of North/South and East/West global interconnectedness. Similar interconnections around climate change, international migration, technology, or conflict/governance/security are oft flagged too. Many development problems and their solutions are neither the preserve of the North/West nor the South/East alone and given international migration, wellbeing in the North/West and South/East is increasingly connected via transnational identities and remittances. Mehta et al. (2006, p. 5) has argued this specifically, that:

> [d]evelopment research should reinvent itself to address the increasing interconnectedness between North and South, local-global linkages, the pedagogy of the powerful, social change in the north, and more genuine interdisciplinarity. Our view is that development research can avoid the same fate of colonial studies and emerge as a way of learning about development and exclusion in both rich and poor countries and lead the way in terms of forging new approaches in connecting global and local issues, policies, solutions, and researchers.

It is important to note that the basis of the universality case is either common characteristics as discussed above or common problems, which we turn to next. While a 'development' lens could be applied universally to all countries, the differences between the GS (albeit bifurcated) and the GN are still so substantial that the basis of doing is contentious. In other words, even if there are some common problems such as adaptation to climate change, those problems manifest in radically different ways. For example, flooding in the UK with house insurance versus flooding in any country in the GS with poor or limited insurance, or relative poverty in the UK versus absolute poverty in country in the GS. This makes the use of the term 'common' problems potentially misleading, as the problems stem from the same source but have very different manifestations. Further, the ability of people and countries to respond is different in the GS versus the GN so it is again questionable to talk of common problems. Another way of thinking about this is that there are common sources of problems, but there are differentiated manifestations and ability to respond in GS and GN.

The recent revitalisation of interest in universality or global development DS in the UK was triggered by Horner and Hulme (2019a), who argued that there has been income convergence and falling global income inequality. Consequentially, DS should stop using the GN/GS binary. They proposed a focus on ‘converging divergence’ and ‘global development’ to replace ‘global convergence’ and ‘international development’. Converging divergence has two dimensions. The first is the convergence of income between the GS and the GN as groups of countries. Second, there is the divergence of income and other substantial inequalities within countries of both the GS and the GN. They also argue that an approach to DS is needed that considers climate change and other common global challenges. Oldekop et al. (2020), building on Hulme and Horner, argue for a shift towards a global DS in response the COVID-19 pandemic's implications. They argue that the pandemic brought to the fore the problem of approaching development as something that happens in the GS. Instead, an approach to development across all countries and their interconnectedness is needed to address similar problems in GN and GS. In a similar vein, Leach et al. (2021; 2024) too argued that the pandemic has exposed the limits of conventional framings of development in DS. They note the universality of the pandemics' impacts and also make the case for global DS.

Such calls for global development have been questioned both in response to Hulme and Horner (see for example, Fischer, 2019) and the ‘pandemic papers’ (written in response to the COVID pandemic) of Oldekop et al. (2020) and Leach et al. (2021). Wiegratz et al. (2023) and Behuria (2025), for example, have questioned the concepts, lenses, and frameworks put forward. Specifically, that at the core of ‘global development’ is a universalistic framing that reduces or diminishes attention to, and thus the importance of, contemporary hierarchies and the history of the global political economy. Wiegratz et al. propose instead re-centring the Global South and that universalistic framings are not suitable for DS, as the global political economy still functions as a hierarchy. They argue that universalising DS ignores the historical inequalities, structural divides, the international division of labour between the North and the South, and between industrialised and non-industrialised countries. They argue that while the shift to ‘global development’ may have noble intentions, it poses several significant challenges and raises concerns. In particular, the potential limiting of development theorising from the GS. The authors argue that the broader trend towards global development tends to overlook the historical origins of development theories and frameworks rooted in the Global South, including the centre-periphery framework that elucidates how Western neo-imperialism perpetuates global inequality. They thus advocate for (re)centring Global South theorists and experiences within DS to understand the economic and political dynamics of contemporary capitalism.

4.3.2 Uncommon Problems?

Are there really 'common' problems? The common problems typically identified by advocates of global development are the commonalities of the meta-trend of climate change, heat, extreme weather events, and the preponderance in the GN and GS of poverty, inequality, and insecurity. However, such issues manifest not only differently in different contexts but also the ability to respond also varies, even in the post-ODA GS versus the GN.

To illustrate: A common starting point in thinking about climate change is exposure to risk and households' capacity to cope. Table 4.1 shows examples of combinations of household exposure to risk and coping capacity and highlights stylised differences between households in the GS and GN. The illustration in Table 4.1 draws on Room (2000) and Wood (2003), who emphasise two key dimensions of the risk–resilience relationship. The first is expected and unexpected variability and in particular the issue of risk exposure. The second refers to resilience capacities and abilities to take opportunities from the situation faced. Given that livelihoods remain central to exiting or remaining in poverty, this observation shifts the balance of attention towards governance in explaining, mediating, and moderating risk exposure and resilience. For example, tenure security, where people live, access to insurance, microcredit, local support networks, and so forth all hinge on governance in a broad sense, i.e., informal and formal. Climate change will increase the frequency and severity of stressors/shocks and such stressors/shocks will be more substantial in the GS due to a larger affected population, less government resources because of lower average income and smaller tax revenues as a share of GDP, less responsive governance, and weaker state capacity compared to the GN. Further, exposure to these stressors/shocks will have a substantial impact among those who already live in or near absolute poverty in the GS.

Exposure to risks from climate change, such as coastal flooding, extreme weather, agriculture productivity, and hunger is also far greater in the GS (see Adom, 2024; Wiebe et al., 2019; CIESIN and CIDR, 2021; EM-DAT, 2024; and Wheeler, 2011). The data shows that an estimated sixty million people in Africa and 500 million in Asia are at risk of sea level rises due to living in low elevation coastal areas. In contrast, the at-risk population in Europe and North America is lower, at forty million in Europe and thirty million in North America. Second, about 1.2 billion people in Africa and 4.5 billion in Asia are exposed to extreme weather due to climate change. For comparison, the

Table 4.1 Examples of household exposure to risk exposure and resilience to cope in the GN and GS

		Resilience	
		Higher	**Lower**
Risk exposure	Higher	Global North example: Highly vulnerable but resilient, e.g., an elderly couple living in a flood-prone neighbourhood but with full health and property insurance, supporting social networks, and excellent emergency services.	Global South example: High vulnerability and low resilience, e.g., an isolated rural community dependent on rain-fed agriculture and with few resources following previous rounds of economic or environmental stress and shock; a community beyond the reach of humanitarian and development aid, perhaps because of conflict.
	Lower	Global North example: Not vulnerable and with high resilience, e.g., a well-resourced family not exposed to current hazards and with sufficient capacity to enjoy flexibility in resource expenditure (i.e., savings), access to knowledge resources to plan, and insurance to cope with unforeseen contingencies and surprises.	Global South example: Not vulnerable but also not resilient, e.g., a household not exposed to current risk, but one that has not been able or is not willing to invest in protecting the household from uncertainty and future contingencies. Investment in education, insurance, and engagement in community governance are not priorities.

Source: Author's elaboration.

at-risk population in Europe is 600 million (and there is no estimate for North America). Third, in Africa, agricultural productivity losses are forecasted to be in the range of 10% to 20% by 2050 (relative to 2008) and the number of people at risk of hunger in sub-Saharan Africa could be close to 200 million. In Asia, productivity losses in agriculture are estimated at 2% to 12% by 2050, while the number of people at risk of hunger could also be over 200 million. To compare, estimated productivity losses in agriculture are 3% in Europe and 2% in North America and the potential numbers at risk of hunger as a consequence are low.

In sum, all parts of the world have a common problem in climate change, but the problem is bigger in the GS and the resources and capacity to cope are smaller. So, whilst it is true to say the GN and GS face the same 'source' of a problem, the exposure to the hazard is generally smaller in the GN in terms of the absolute population affected. Furthermore, the ability to respond and the strength of institutions is weaker in the Global South. Furthermore, the capacity to cope is much higher in the GN relative to the GS. There is a further contention with universality, namely that is the GN controls the prospects for development in the GS. We turn to this next.

4.4 The Prospects for Development

The issue of who holds sway over the prospects for development is important because it is the clearest indication of the persistence of Seers' special case. The GN continues to wield considerable clout over the global economic hierarchy, encompassing the international political economy, and thus the prospects for the GS. It is difficult to deliberate upon common problems or the universality of development while the GN maintains its authority and influence global governance (i.e., the IMF and the World Bank who provide resources to deal with the global challenges like climate change) and the global economy (through the lead TNCs and financial institutions).

The theoretical argument for the special case resembles the core/periphery concepts of structuralism and the concept of late development, wherein the prospects for national economic development in the GS are shaped and constrained by factors controlled by the GN, such as the GN's transnational corporations, the GN's control of global finance, and global governance. The determinants of structural transformation in developing nations, including commodity prices, exchange rate differentials, interest rate differentials, access to global value chains, and the role of the activist state, are all influenced by global factors to varying extents, leaving much of the GS with limited economic autonomy. As noted in Chapter 3, the situation is particularly exacerbated by the fragmentation of global production into global value chains (GVCs) since the Cold War. While GS countries can still achieve structural transformation, it may be more difficult than in the past, and newer pathways of structural transformation such as tertiarisation may occur at lower levels of per capita income than earlier developers experienced, with implications for employment growth, real wage growth, and value-added. Despite significant economic growth in many developing countries, substantial and sustained economic development and structural transformation may remain elusive, particularly in the ODA-dependent GS that struggles to initiate industrialisation. And in the post-ODA GS, sustaining the transition towards higher value-added activities and employment may also be tough, as many middle-income developing countries as noted are experiencing stalling industrialisation or premature deindustrialisation (see Felipe et al., 2014; Palma 2005; 2008; Rodrik, 2016; Sumner, 2021). Specifically, the expansion of their manufacturing base has stalled because of liberalised trade and increased competition in global value chains. The consequent thin spread of manufacturing jobs across many countries makes it hard for individual countries to sustain high levels of manufacturing employment. To reiterate, the Felipe et al. (2019) argument is important. Specifically, that achieving a high-income status is associated with a country reaching a certain level of peak manufacturing employment, which relatively few, if any, developing countries today are likely to attain. This raises important questions about how to make manufacturing-led economic development more viable or alternatively, whether modern services sector-led growth can generate sufficient, widely distributed, and well-paid employment and value added in the GS, given the technological shifts of recent years and generative AI (which raises questions about the scope for mass employment generation through tradable services). In other words, the global economy and the international division of labour in fragmented global value chains significantly impact the economic development of both ODA-dependent and post-ODA GS countries.

To achieve economic development and structural transformation and thus to become a developed country in a GVC world, higher value-added activities such as research and development (R and D), design, distribution, and advertising are needed. However, these are typically concentrated in the GN and controlled by GN transnational corporations (TNCs), whereas lower value-added activities such as manufacturing, assembly, and retail/sales are more likely to be found in the GS. These factors can 'lock-in' GS countries, making it tough to upgrade within GVCs. The GS exception to this China. China has many TNCs or lead TNCs in GVCs. However, beyond China, it is the TNCs of the GN that control the value chains of primary commodities, manufacturing, and the service sectors, which companies in the GS act as suppliers to. GVC participation initially can provide some employment and value-added to low-income countries (see Pahl and Timmer, 2020) though this becomes difficult to sustain as labour costs rise over time and more countries compete for similar GVC entry points. As a result, as outlined in Chapter 3, developing countries are increasingly pursuing a form of economic development that loses momentum around middle-income levels. In this shallow economic development, only a small number of globally competitive domestic companies in each country are integrated into global value chains and there is no longer a focus on building deep economic development through extensive domestic industries. Modern technology can be utilised through participation in global value chains, although this often involves non-ownership or borrowing on unfavourable terms that must be paid for through patents and fee expenses. Moreover, developing countries have limited control over the governance of contemporary GVCs, as they are often relegated to a semi-periphery status within the GVC world given lead TNCs are typically headquartered in GN countries.

It must be noted that this narrative pertains to an average developing country. It is conceivable that a single country or a few countries could capture most of the value-added and employment, thereby achieving economic progress, although potentially at the expense of other GS nations. However, competition among developing countries for a share of lower-productivity activities within GVCs will ultimately result in downward pressure on the prices of manufacturing exports generated by these activities, which will in turn reduce wages. This will lead to growth characterised by a declining labour share and weak formal sector employment creation. Furthermore, developing countries are typically excluded from the more lucrative tasks within GVCs since these tasks are already dominated by GN countries. In short, the advantages of participating in global value chains are apparent for low-income countries, though they may diminish for middle-income countries (see Pahl and Timmer, 2020). In contrast, GVC participation is advantageous for high-income countries, as leading companies from these countries capitalise on low-income or middle-income countries through their oligopolistic market power. Consequently, a new form of dependency or subordination of the Global South is evident.

4.5 Conclusion

In conclusion, this chapter has focused on the scope of development and thus the scope of Development Studies. It has been argued that pursuing universality, meaning to dispense with the GS/GN differentiation, risks losing sight of the key structural constraints to any kind of development for the GS. While there has been some convergence of income for post-ODA GS countries, structural convergence is much less evident apart from a set of East Asian countries and China in particular. Some challenges may be common, while others are specific to the GS or of a qualitatively or quantitatively different nature. In other words, the exposure to the common challenge is different in nature. Further, the capacity to respond in terms of financial resources or human capital is quite different.

We can conclude with the following: First, that GS and GN countries remain different, even post-ODA GS countries. While development can be applied universally to all countries, the differences between the GS, albeit bifurcated between ODA-dependent and post-ODA, and the GN remain so substantial that it is questionable to do so. To talk about convergence is also meaningless except when considering China and perhaps a handful of GS countries. Furthermore, how meaningful it is if the process that could take 100 years or much longer is open to question. Average income is a poor reflection of structural characteristics and it would take a long time to converge in an absolute sense, begging the question of how useful it is to focus on income convergence. Second, common problems manifest quite differently, and the ability to respond varies. Even if some problems are common, such as adaptation to climate change, those problems manifest in such radically different way that the use of the term 'common' problems is questionable. The problems are the same source but manifest differently, which is exacerbated by different capacities to respond at the household and government level. Third, the GN continues to hold power in the global political economy and controls the prospects for development. In the post-ODA GS, the GN still controls the development prospects through the GN's lead transnational corporations (TNCs), international organisations, and the structure and nature of global markets. Hence, what is needed to foster economic development and structural transformation and become a developed country in a GVC world, higher value-added activities, still tends to be concentrated in developed countries, while lower value-added activities are more likely to be in the GS. There are a handful of exceptions of GS countries that have powerful TNCs in global value chains, for example, China. However, the GN also still controls the governance and decision-making of key international institutions, institutionally through voting structures at the IMF and World Bank. In sum, there is persistence in Seers' special case. The GN is different. Even in parts of the GS that are post-ODA, countries still retain many of the structural characteristics of developing countries outlined by Seers many years ago.

5
Continuum III
The Onto-Epistemology of Development

Development and its Discontents. Andy Sumner, Oxford University Press. © Andy Sumner (2026).
DOI: 10.1093/9780198902904.003.0005

5.1 Introduction

In the previous chapters, we discussed the framing of development and the scope of development. In this chapter, we turn to the onto-epistemology of development. The modes of thought in Development Studies differ sometimes radically not only in their framing and scope of development but also in their onto-epistemology of development. This discussion relates closely to Bevan's knowledge foundations and specifically different ideas of what politics and power are and how they manifest. This chapter asks what the world is assumed to be like. Further, how do different onto-epistemological perspectives relate to understandings of power and politics? These questions pose a particular challenge to Development Studies given its cross-disciplinary nature.

This chapter argues that different ways of understanding and knowing the world need to be brought to the fore as they constitute an important difference between scholars in Development Studies. Second, it is argued that anti-imperialism and decolonisation are both material and epistemic. Development Studies should pursue intellectual decolonisation but remain robust in its critique, too, on the material political economy dimensions of imperialism and anti-imperialism.

The chapter is structured as follows: Section 2 discusses what is meant by onto-epistemology. Section 3 highlights how onto-epistemological perspectives shape the central concepts of power and politics across disciplines and, thus, across modes and schools of thought in Development Studies. Section 4 then illustrates using the discussion of intellectual and material decolonisation/anti-imperialism and the pluralisation of Development Studies itself beyond Anglo-Saxon-dominated scholarship. Section 5 concludes the chapter.

5.2 Ontology, Epistemology, and Development Studies

5.2.1 Onto-Epistemology

Ontology and epistemology are two fundamental concepts that address questions regarding the nature of reality and how social reality can be known.[1] However, considering how foundational these concepts are, they are surprisingly little discussed in Development Studies. In fact, many differences

[1] This section builds on the earlier discussion of Sumner and Tribe (2008).

between the schools of thought in Development Studies stem from radically different ontological and epistemological assumptions embedded in different social science disciplines.

It is useful to clarify definitions at the outset. Ontology is concerned with the nature of social reality. By contrast, epistemology considers how we know about reality. Clearly, perceptions of social reality determine to a large extent what can be known about that social reality (or what humans think they can know). Furthermore, both concepts require assumptions that are impossible to prove or disprove. Ontology deals with what the world is assumed to be like. Epistemology is a set of assumptions about how a human can 'know' reality.

Onto-epistemological questions have a long history that is important to reflect on too. Questions regarding the essence, implications, and fundamentals of knowledge have been a significant focus of philosophical enquiry since at least Plato's Theaetetus dialogue (360 BCE). Such reflections include Descartes' 'search for certainty', which implied that anything subject to doubt cannot be deemed 'truth'. There was also the competition to identify a 'criterion of truth' between Greek sceptics, the Stoics, and the Epicureans. Other examples are Leibniz's and Kant's 'principles of sufficient reason' or the notion that everything has an underlying cause. In all these discussions, the central conceptual issue is what is 'knowable'. Or the extent to which humans can 'know' anything. Further, how humans should evaluate claims to 'know'. Socrates, Plato, and Aristotle. They argued that the basis of knowledge was the inductive method, or that generalisations were drawn from the evidence.

A second strand is the rise of empiricism during the oft referred to 'birth of reason'. This period entailed radical questioning of religious or mythical explanations of phenomena. It thus triggered the contemplation of the social as well as physical world, leading to rapid shifts in thinking about knowledge and human progress as based in 'scientific' beliefs rather than religious beliefs. This shift was also about proclaiming the individual to be autonomous and separate from nature or God, which had dominated knowledge prior to this period. This era is associated with Bacon, Locke, Hume, and Mill, who argued that the foundation of knowledge was observation or empiricism, proposing the application of scientific and mathematical principles to social reality. Galileo, Hobbes, and Descartes posited that mathematics provided the foundations of knowledge and applied a deductive rather than inductive method, using theory as a basis for generalising. By the 1700s, there was a growing view that knowledge should be acquired through empirical or observational methods, and through mathematics. In this period of intellectual ferment, the foundations were laid of many academic disciplines that exist today, such as economics and politics.

This view of knowledge as emerging during the European Enlightenment appears Eurocentric. It was, though, shaped by ideas from other regions. Each family of epistemology can be found in both western and non-western scholarship. Islamic scholars such as Averroes (Ibn Rushd) and Avicenna (Ibn Sina) made contributions to logic, metaphysics, and medicine that shaped medieval European scholasticism. The transmission of Islamic advances in mathematics, astronomy, and medicine had been reaching Europe through centuries of cultural and intellectual exchange well before the Enlightenment took place. Indian mathematical contributions, including the decimal system and the concept of zero, were transmitted to Europe through Islamic scholarly networks and incorporated into European scientific practice. Chinese political and ethical thought influenced Enlightenment thinkers too. Voltaire praised the rational philosophy and meritocratic governance of Chinese civilisation in his *Essai sur les mœurs*. Leibniz engaged with Chinese thought in his *Novissima Sinica* (1697) and *Discourse on the Natural Theology of the Chinese* (1715/16), interpreting ancient Confucian concepts through a Christian Platonic lens and arguing that Chinese philosophy contained a natural theology compatible with Christianity. The Jesuit missions in China played a considerable role in this intellectual exchange. They introduced European thinkers to Chinese philosophical traditions and systems of governance, shaping wider discussions on rational ethics and natural morality. African knowledge systems also contributed. Scholars at centres of learning such as Timbuktu's Sankoré mosque-university engaged in philosophical, theological, and legal inquiry long before the colonial period, though their direct influence operated primarily within Islamic and African intellectual networks. Indigenous American intellectuals shaped European debates too. Graeber and Wengrow (2021) argue that the Wendat statesman Kandiaronk (also rendered Kondiaronk) articulated pointed critiques of European hierarchy and social inequality that reached Enlightenment thinkers through Lahontan's *Dialogues* (1703), though this thesis remains contested among historians. In sum, the Enlightenment was not a European phenomenon alone. It drew on global intellectual exchanges, some spanning several centuries including Islamic, Chinese, Indian, African, and Indigenous American thought.

This wider context points towards the fact that although the Enlightenment is often referred to as the period of ferment and progress in human thinking, the birth of science, and rationality or (one idea of) 'modernity', there are multiple modernities. Some refer to modernity as the centralised bureaucratic power or nation states; others to intellectual development, the use of science and technology, and rationality; and yet others to industrial development. Some of these modernities existed thousands of years before European modernity, even though modernity existed alongside anti-modernity thinking, as was also the case in Europe too. Modernity need not necessarily be defined as a purely European or Western concept (Eisenstadt, 2000). Evidence of various aspects of modernity such as a centralised state, bureaucratic administration, and scientific progress can be found in the 'cradles of civilisation' of Ancient India, China, and Egypt, as well as Mesopotamia, the Caral-Supe in Peru, and the Olmec in Mexico. Each of these pre-dates the Renaissance by thousands of years.

The onto-epistemology most closely associated with the Enlightenment is Positivism. Figures such as Locke, Hume, and Mill contributed to positivism through their focus on empiricism, whilst rationalist thinkers such as Hobbes, Descartes, and Spinoza contributed to the broader Enlightenment intellectual climate through their use of mathematical and deductive reasoning. Comte is often regarded as the founder of positivism in the social sciences, given he was among the first to argue that the scientific method used in the physical sciences should also be applied in the social sciences. This meant not only observation but also experimentation. In the 1920s and 1930s, positivism evolved into logical positivism, or logical empiricism, among a group of philosophers known as the 'Vienna Circle'. This group included Otto Neurath, Rudolf Carnap, Kurt Gödel, Friedrich Waismann, and Moritz Schlick. It is Ayer's (1936) book that is considered the core publication for the anglophone reception of logical positivism.

Ayer distinguished between strong and weak verification. However, strong or fully conclusive verification is not possible for an empirical proposition because it depends on further experience.[2] Popper was associated with the Vienna Circle but held a slightly different perspective. He contended that the central issue is identifying the boundary between science and 'non-science'. A theory is 'scientific' if it can be tested. Scientists should seek to falsify their hypotheses rather than verifying them. Therefore, all hypotheses should be falsifiable by observation.

[2] Logical positivism asserts that there are two methods to attain knowledge: through logical reasoning and through empirical evidence for assessing verifiable propositions. Logical reasoning entails deducing information a priori or without relying on experience, whereas empirical evidence is derived from observable facts or a posteriori. Logical positivists posited that scientific statements should be subjected to verification or the 'principle of verification' and that scientific research must adhere to the natural or physical science model, including the method of observing phenomena.

Although Positivism is often associated with Western scholars, there were broader intellectual influences or parallels in many non-Western scholarly traditions or development of similar ideas. For example, Islamic scholars placed emphasis on empirical observation and systematic inquiry. Alhazen (Ibn al-Haytham) was a pioneer in optics and the scientific method, advocating rigorous experimentation and observation and presenting ideas of hypothesis testing and replicable experiments. Avicenna (Ibn Sina) contributed to early classifications of knowledge grounded in rationalism and empirical observation (Gutas, 2014), and Averroes (Ibn Rushd) similarly engaged in systematic inquiry into the rational foundations of knowledge. Chinese scholars developed sophisticated systems for classifying and organising knowledge, though these operated within intellectual frameworks distinct from European positivism. In classical Indian philosophy, the Nyāya school advocated logic, inference, and empirical verification that resonate with positivist epistemology. Pre-colonial African scholarly traditions, such as those associated with Timbuktu, incorporated empirical methods in medicine, astronomy, and legal studies, and indigenous American societies, notably the Maya, Aztec, and Inca civilisations, engaged in extensive empirical study in fields such as astronomy, agriculture, and medicine. Such convergences suggest that systematic, observation-based reasoning emerged across diverse civilisations independently of European intellectual lineages, complicating straightforward narratives of positivism as an exclusively Western tradition.

In the 1900s, however, Positivism was challenged by Nietzsche, Foucault, Kuhn, Said, and others who questioned the tenet of positivism, the existence of absolute truth, and argued that knowledge was constructed or relative rather than discovered or 'absolute'. This was duly labelled relativism. This is a completely different view of social reality and what can be known. This perspective is also associated with Berger, Derrida, Latour, and Luckmann, who emphasised the social construction of knowledge and meaning based on the idea that social reality is not independent from human experience. In fact, they argued that that multiple realities exist. There is no single 'truth'. Any claims to know with certainty are to be treated as suspicious. In the words of later scholars of this tradition, 'there are no absolute truths and no objective values' (Rue, 1994, pp. 272–273). This illustrates how relativism is best understood as a reaction to modernity's certainties of rationality, faith in progress, and science and positivisms embodiment of these. The goal of relativist research is a more informed, sophisticated, and inclusive construction of the world given that it is argued that universalistic claims tend to marginalise those who do not fit. In sum, positivism and relativism are diametrically opposed views on what constitutes reality and knowledge about reality. Debates about relativism have had diverse influences or parallel discussions across the globe. In Islamic philosophy, Al-Ghazālī questioned the philosophers' claims to certain knowledge and stressed the limits of reason (Griffel, 2009). Ibn Khaldūn treated knowledge and norms as historically and socially situated (Ibn Khaldūn, 1958). In Indian philosophical traditions, Jain *anekāntavāda* holds that no single perspective captures the whole of truth (Matilal, 1981; Dundas, 2002). Chinese philosophy too engaged with relativism, and the *Zhuāngzǐ* is read as endorsing perspectivalism (Fraser, 2014; 2024).

Realists are between the two camps of positivism and relativism and seek to argue that there is an independent reality and an empirical reality that can be observed. However, the real meaning and structures may or may not be 'actualised'. 'Realism' is rooted in the work of Locke and Descartes, who contended that there is a knowable reality independent of humans, but our perceptions of it are subjective. The positivist position leans towards objective reality, whereas the relativist position leans towards subjective reality and realism asserts that reality exists independent of human perception but can only be known subjectively. Realism too has non-western associations, influences, and parallels. In Islamic philosophy, Ibn Sina (Avicenna) developed a distinction between 'essence' and 'existence' that carries realist implications for ontology, positing that the external world has a structure independent of human cognition (Gutas, 2014). Al-Farabi and Averroes (Ibn Rushd) similarly affirmed the reality of an external world independent of human perception. In classical Indian philosophy, the Nyāya school developed a programme of logic and inquiry grounded in four *pramāṇas* (perception, inference, comparison, and testimony) as articulated in the *Nyāya Sūtra* attributed to Gautama; the school is widely characterised in the secondary literature as committed to a form of metaphysical realism. In African philosophical traditions, the Akan tradition, as analysed by Gyekye (1995), places significant emphasis on communal dimensions of inquiry and practical wisdom. While this does not reduce cognitive truth to collective agreement, it reflects an epistemology in which social experience and intersubjective deliberation are integral. In Chinese philosophy, Daoist thought, as exemplified by Zhuangzi, interrogates the limitations of human perception with an emphasis is on the fluidity and relativity of perspectives (Fraser, 2024).

The distinctions between positivism, relativism, and realism can be further discerned (see Table 5.1) by direct comparison of foundational assumptions related to the nature of reality, the objective of research, and the reality-researcher relationship. For example, by evaluating whether research seeks

Table 5.1 Onto-epistemological traditions and foundational assumptions

	Foundational assumptions		
	The nature of reality	**The objective of research**	**The relationship between reality and the research/er**
Positivist tradition	There is one, observable reality.	Acquisition of a single, universal truth or law.	The researcher is objective and independent of the researched.
Realist tradition	There is a reality which exists independently of the researcher.	To describe reality.	The researcher is a dependent observer.
Relativist tradition	There are multiple realities, which can be experienced or interpreted.	A construction of meaning or understanding.	The researcher is subjective and not independent of the researched.

Source: Adapted from Sumner and Tribe (2008, p. 59).

a singular truth (positivism), multiple truths (relativism), or something in between (realism). Positivism is related to certainty, while relativism accentuates a more knowledgeable comprehension of reality; realism lies somewhere in the middle.

Positivism is based on the idea that there is an objective reality; that reality can be accessed through observation; that reality is unambiguous. It is measurable; and there is independence between reality, the researcher, and the instruments of research (none may influence any other). In contrast, relativism is based on the notion that there are multiple realities; that reality can be experienced; reality is ambiguous and non-measurable. This means only an informed construction or understanding is possible; and the researcher is subjective and not independent of the researched. Finally, realism posits that there is an existing reality, which can be described and is independent of the researcher. However, it is not possible to establish 'truth' about that reality. Furthermore, the researcher and their thoughts are part of that reality. Therefore, the researcher is a dependent observer.

In the social sciences, such discussions remain heavily influenced by the 'battle for science' or 'science wars' of the 1960s. This was fuelled by Kuhn's (1962) critique of science, Feyerabend's (1975) 'epistemological anarchism' (that there is no single way of acquiring knowledge that is to be privileged), and Popper's (1959) defence of science. Kuhn argued that science is ideological, value-laden, and driven by whatever the dominant ideas are within the scientific community or the 'disciplinary matrix'. And Kuhn argued that each scientific community has a set of 'beliefs, values, and techniques' (p. 175). These are shared by the members of the community. Different schools then compete over this 'worldview'. Kuhn, in keeping with the relativist position, argued that truth is simply a product of the dominant paradigm and scientists are not objective. Rather, anomalies build up against the hegemonic theory during 'normal science' and eventually lead to a scientific revolution or a new theory or worldview. Kuhn's interest was in how ideas are 'thinkable'. He argued that the main cause of paradigm shifts is the turnover in the membership of scientists in each generation. Kuhn (1962, p. 150) put it thus:

> Practising in different worlds, the two groups of scientists see different things when they look from the same point in the same direction.

In contrast, Popper's (1959) focus distinguishing between 'science' and 'non-science' in the social sciences led him to argue that only testable and falsifiable theories can be 'scientific'. Human knowledge is constantly evolving. No scientific statement can ever be proven beyond doubt.

Why does the entire preceding discussion matter to Development Studies? In Development Studies, researchers need to be cognizant of their presuppositions regarding the nature of reality, objectives of knowledge enquiry, and relationship between themselves and the subjects of their research. Why? Because such aspects are already embedded in each of the constituent discipline in Development Studies and their worldview and ultimately influence the process and outcomes of research.

5.2.2 Development Studies and the Onto-Epistemology of Development

Development Studies, like all studies in the social sciences, is influenced by understandings about the nature of reality and knowledge. Hence, in Chapter 2, we referred to major trends in the social sciences. The assumptions humans have about any concepts shape how humans select, interpret, and frame attempts to 'know' anything through research. Furthermore, such ontological and epistemological assumptions are rooted in human beings' own ontological and epistemological beliefs, values, and assumptions of social reality (see Chambers, 2005; Molteberg and Bergstrøm, 2000a; 2000b).

The consequences of these debates on conducting research in a cross-disciplinary field such as Development Studies are substantial. Different disciplines may be dominant, even within cross-disciplinary approaches (Hulme and Toye, 2007). Often, there are diverse assumptions about ontology, which subsequently influence epistemological strategies and shape choices of theorising, methodologies, and methods. Harriss (2002) illustrates this well for Development Studies by noting the role of anthropologists in challenging conventional wisdom by focusing on understandings of poverty of those living in poverty. However, Harriss also points to the problem that different disciplinary perspectives often talk past each other. Kanbur and Shaffer (2007) highlight too diverse lenses on poverty. They show how differences in the study of poverty manifest in several distinct ways. First, different epistemologies have implications for how data is transformed numerically, how validity is judged, what the actual concept of poverty is, as well as interpersonal comparisons. Second, they illustrate that thinking about poverty as a consumption-based phenomenon is inherently empiricist and privileges what they call 'brute data', based on the assumption that poverty as intersubjectively observable and 'subject-invariant'. In contrast, more anthropological approaches are inherently situated in the tradition of hermeneutics or intersubjective meanings that arise from dialogue. In other words, claims to 'knowledge' may often be non-comparable.

Some constituent disciplinary approaches within Development Studies, such as economics, strive for objectivity akin to the physical sciences. Others, such as anthropology, adopt different perspectives. McGregor (2007) notes, echoing Bevan (2007), how each discipline has its own concepts, vocabularies, and foundational assumptions. Thus, it is important for researchers to recognise underlying assumptions and how these assumptions ultimately impact what they 'see' and 'know' in terms of their research findings and conclusions. This is because ontology and epistemology are intertwined, framing and shaping research design, execution, and outcome.

It is not difficult to identify the positivist tradition within Development Studies. This is evident in the classical development economics within classical Development Studies. Positivism and empirical science firmly believe in the power of scientific discovery, the accuracy and certainty of scientific methods, and the idea that objects possess meaning independent of human consciousness. At the same time, Relativism too is clear in contemporary Development Studies. Relativist thinking has been influential in the post-development and decolonial school which posits that there are no absolute truths or impartial values, and that truth claims often exclude marginalised groups as a form of power or control. There are multiple ambiguous realities or a 'pluriverse' with varying meanings for each interpreter, and no separation between the perception of reality, researcher, researched, and instruments of research.

All of this discussion brings us back to the issue that numerous fundamental theoretical concepts in the social sciences and in Development Studies have never been directly observed. Yet they remain heuristic devices. Researchers in Development Studies must thus continually grapple with questions of onto-epistemology that underpin their assumptions about social reality and knowledge. One illustration of this is how different conceptualisations of power and politics manifest themselves across disciplines. This chapter turns to this illustration next.

5.3 Power and Politics in Development Studies

Different understandings of power and politics illustrate the differences in onto-epistemological approaches across disciplines in the social sciences. They also do so in Development Studies itself. There are at some very different approaches to understanding power (referring to the ability to control or influence others or having power 'over' others) and its sources and mechanics. In other words, there are multiple ways to conceptualise politics.

Lasswell (1936, p. 1) defines politics as the study of 'influence and the influential'. It asks what power is and how it is contested within and between countries. In material political economy, as outlined by Marx and those writing in a Marxist tradition, power is based on socio-economic relationships, social groups, and structures between and within countries. In contrast, power can also be about discourses and knowledge or how ideas/narratives are constructed and embedded with power dynamics. The discursive or epistemic approach to power is elucidated by Said, Foucault, and somewhat, Bourdieu in different ways. The commonality is that the mechanisms of power are not based on simple coercion and hierarchy but are more subtle and internalised by the dominated, often relating to representations of the 'Other'. Further, power can also be embedded in institutions. As North (1990, p. 3) put it, institutions are 'the rules of the game in a society, or, more formally, the humanly devised constraints that shape human interaction'. Power then manifests in institution which are 'any collectively accepted system of rules (procedures, practices)' (Searle, 2005, p. 21). Hence, power is shaped by who sets the formal or informal 'rules' and who benefits or not from those rules. In that sense, power is the ability to frame and shape formal and informal institutions and thus hold power over others. Various scholars have offered approaches to understanding the sources of power. Their prominence largely depends on the respective discipline. For instance, in sociology, one can identify Said (e.g., 1978, 1983; 1993), Foucault (e.g., 1970; 1972; 1977; 1980; 1991), and Bourdieu (e.g., 1984; 1986; 1989; 1990). In politics, heterodox economics, and political economy, one can note Marx (e.g., 1867) and those following that tradition (for example, Amin, 1974; 1976; 1977; 1980; 1990; Wallerstein, 1974a, 1980; 1989; 2011). Further, in various disciplines, there are iterations of North's (e.g., 1990, 1991, 2005a; 2005b) institutions or older institutionalism such as the historical (Mahoney and Thelen, 2009) or sociological (Hall and Taylor, 1996) that each emphasise the role of institutions albeit in different ways.

We can compare further each of these. The discussions in previous chapters touched upon the subject of discourse and power, drawing on the work of Said in particular. To recap, Said drew selectively on Foucault's theory of discursive power. Foucault (1980) contended that power and knowledge are inseparable. Further, that each historical epoch is governed by a deep epistemic structure (an 'épistème') or discourse that invisibly determines the conditions of possibility for all knowledge within it and the regularities that govern what statements can be made, by whom, and under what conditions (Foucault, 1970; 1972; 1980). Power thus pertains to the creation and distribution of knowledge and the formation of narratives that shape human understanding of the world and imply hierarchies of status. As noted, Said's (1978; 1983; 1993) analysis centred on the concept of 'Orientalism', which has historically depicted the East or non-Western countries as inferior and backward. According to Said, this discourse served to legitimise of domination, justifying imperialism and neo-imperialism through 'Othering', which involves the West defining itself in opposition to a dehumanised and imagined 'Other' of the non-West. This is achieved by producing and using knowledge to build dominant discourses and cultural representations. The latter assert the West's superiority and legitimacy while marginalising and silencing alternative voices and perspectives. In short, discursive power operates to colonise and hold power 'over' the Global South (GS) by utilising Western knowledge, representations, and narratives to legitimise control of the GS.

Foucault's notion of power underlies Said to some extent. Foucault's (1970; 1972; 1977; 1980; 1991) thinking concentrated on the productive and regulatory aspects of power within a discourse and institutions. Foucault emphasises the diffuse nature of power and posits that it operates through a web of discourses, practices, and institutions beyond Said's notion of power in some ways. One of Foucault's (1991) core concepts is 'governmentality', which refers to the way one group can govern and subordinate others within a specific political order. This is achieved by 'disciplining' subjects who conform to political order and internalise the values of the order and thus become docile, governable bodies (Foucault referred to Bentham's panopticon of self-policing). Foucauldian power thus operates in the GS through forms of conduct that align with the prevailing ideology and institutions of the GN (and the underlying knowledge that legitimises this) and/or elites of the GS who have taken on the ideology as their own.

In contemporary Development Studies, the discourse tradition of thinking about power encompasses several strands. Said's (1978; 1983; 1993) 'Orientalism' argues that the West constructs representations of the 'Other' to legitimise colonial power. Spivak's (1988; 1999) view is that power operates through silencing the 'subaltern'. Fanon's (1952; 1961; 1967) analysis is that power operates through cultural domination. Ndlovu-Gatsheni's (2013; 2018) position is that power in the post-colonial world is structured by colonial logic. De Sousa Santos (2007; 2014) argues that power is exercised through knowledge hierarchies.

Relatedly, Bourdieu's (1984; 1986; 1989; 1990) concepts of cultural capital and habitus argue that power is embedded in social practices and internalised dispositions. Bourdieu (1986) contends that capital exists in three principal forms (economic, cultural, and social) and that the unequal distribution of these forms across social space is the primary mechanism through which privilege is accumulated. 'Symbolic' power operates by making these objective social hierarchies appear natural and legitimate. For example, aesthetic taste reflects and reproduces class position through the internalised logic of 'the habitus' which is a system of durable, transposable dispositions acquired through experience (Bourdieu, 1984; 1989; 1990). Bourdieu thus argues that power operates through symbolic representation or cultural capital. This means that the powerful hold cultural and symbolic capital, which legitimises their power over those who do not possess these forms of capital. In short, the GS or the non-elites in the GS do not own the capital that the GN or GS elites hold. A central concept in Bourdieu's analysis is that of the 'habitus', which refers to the internalisation of such perceptions of inferiority as well as preferences and views that individuals acquire through socialisation in specific contexts. Habitus shapes people's behaviour to reproduce existing power relations. In the context of GS, it might be argued that the training of many senior civil servants in the GS at GN universities could shape their internalised perceptions and preferences for following and reproducing Western modernity. Cultural capital, specifically, education, knowledge, preferences, and tastes, is then utilised by dominant groups in the GS to assert symbolic power, legitimising the power of those who possess cultural capital and marginalising those who do not. These power relations are reproduced through the internalisation of dominant norms and practices in populations in the GS.

In contrast to these approaches, scholars writing in the Marxist tradition, and influenced by Marx's concept of power at a national and international level, are clearly evident in Development Studies. The tradition of thinking about power encompasses Marx's (1867) concept of power as rooted in economic relations and ideological structures, whereby the capitalist mode of production determines social relations and class struggle. The tradition emphasises the role of power in economic relationships and class dynamics at different scales. Power is rooted in the ownership of capital and means of production, leading to the exploitation of the working classes by the bourgeoisie. This concept of power extends to the GS, where the exploitation of the GS by the GN is seen as a manifestation of power through the hierarchy of the global economy. The mechanisms of power include ownership of capital and oligopolistic market structure, both on global and national scales.

This materialist perspective extends to both Marxist and non-Marxist structuralists and dependency theorists. Amin's (1974; 1976) dependency and unequal-exchange argument holds that peripheral economies are structurally subordinated to the core within global capitalism. In a related but non-Marxist tradition, Prebisch (1950 [1949]) argues that asymmetries between developed and developing countries persist due to long-run trade and investment patterns that favour the core. While there is a clear influence of Marx, along with classical political economists such as Ricardo and Smith, many approaches within the dependency and structuralist traditions are not necessarily neomarxist. Rather, they incorporate elements of historical materialism while also emphasising the agency of states and peripheral economies in navigating global economic structures (Kay, 1989). These perspectives highlight that power is not only about economic relations but also about the institutional frameworks that regulate these relations, reinforcing or challenging existing hierarchies in the global economy.

Finally, North's (1990) approach to power emphasises the role of formal and informal institutions, such as rules, norms, and organisations, in shaping human interactions. The work of early institutionalists in historical institutionalism and sociological institutionalism also points in this direction. Institutionalists believe that institutions shape behaviour and mediate power relations between groups and individuals. For example, 'good' economic policy is defined as market-based and open economies. This is as defined by the International Monetary Fund (IMF), World Bank, and World Trade Organization (WTO). Formal and informal institutions can encompass a wide range of arrangements, including legal regimes, property rights, and organisational structures. All of these influence incentives and constraints on certain groups and determine where power lies in a country or globally, if applied to international organisations. These institutions act as scaffolding for a global political order and determine how resources are allocated (i.e., concessional finance). They also define the rules of acceptable or 'good' policy, extending to what the 'Washington Consensus' was, i.e., not just market-based, open economies but also fiscal balance. It is important to note that institutions are not static (neither are other forms of power, e.g., dominant discourses may shift over time) and may evolve due to factors such as technological change, which can lead to shifts in power within society or globally. North's (1990) writing within the new institutionalist tradition conceptualises institutions as humanly devised constraints that structure political, economic, and social interactions. In this view, power operates through the design and enforcement of institutions that govern economic activity, where institutions can be inclusive, promoting broad participation and long-term development, or extractive, consolidating wealth and control among elites, as Acemoglu and Robinson (2012) argue.

In sum, there are multiple ways of thinking about the power and politics relevant to Development Studies. For example, discourse-based approaches are visible in the post-development/decolonial school and assertions that power operates via the control of representations of the GS and the internalisation of power by those who are dominated. On the other hand, material political economy approaches in Classical Development Studies posit that power operates through socio-economic relationships, such as ownership of production and the role of classes or groups of people or countries, conceptualised nationally or internationally. Alternatively, other schools of thought in Development Studies consider power and politics to be yielded more through institutional arrangements and practices in society. 'Problem Solving' Development Studies or global Development Studies may apply such approaches, though other approaches to power may also be evident. All the above matters to Development Studies because these differing perspectives on power significantly influence the understanding of development. One way to explore this further is to consider discussions within Development Studies on the subject of 'decolonisation'.

5.4 Decolonisation and Development Studies

One way to illustrate these ontological and epistemological differences in Development Studies and the broader social sciences is to consider both discursive or epistemic and materialist perspectives on decolonisation and anti-imperialism. This helps explain different understandings of power dynamics and politics.

As Behuria and Sumner (2025) note, calls to decolonise knowledge are evident not only in Development Studies but across the social sciences and beyond. Such calls have grown louder over time (e.g., Escobar, 1992; 1995; 2007; Melber et al., 2024; Mignolo, 2002; Quijano, 2000; Patel, 2020; Pailey, 2020 and for a different perspective, Táíwò, 2022). To reiterate, a useful demarcation to make at the outset is that of Hull (2021) who differentiates between 'decoloniality' and 'intellectual decolonisation' (see also, Hull, 2019; 2022). The former draws on anticolonial and post-colonial critiques and argues that many Western representations of the Global South are historically embedded in power/knowledge formations that reproduce racialised hierarchies and Eurocentrism, often legitimating 'modernisation' as development during and after colonial rule (see Césaire, 2000; Fanon, 1952; 1961; Said, 1978; 1983; 1993). The second concept addresses the broadening of knowledge production beyond scholarship dominated by North American and European traditions, typically framed within the conventions of scientific inquiry. One position holds that this amounts to an acknowledgment of theoretical contributions from researchers in the Global South. A more radical interpretation treats this as 'intellectual decolonisation': a substantive transformation of teaching and research away from the assumed authority of Northern perspectives, underpinned by meaningful institutional reform to challenge entrenched racial hierarchies in academic life, and by the cultivation of equitable international scholarly partnerships. Others argue that there should be a much wider discussion of what counts as knowledge, not restricted to articles published in scientific journals. Instead, they argue that there is no hierarchy of 'scientific' knowledge over 'non-scientific' knowledge (see Ndlovu-Gatsheni, 2018; Santos, 2007; 2014; Escobar, 2007).

In short, approaches to 'decolonisation' vary. Some scholars prioritise epistemic decolonisation, challenging the perpetuation of stereotypes, exoticisation, and the undermining of non-Western knowledge systems. Others focus on material political economy, scrutinising trade imbalances, debt burdens, and resource inequalities as mechanisms of oppression. While clearly many scholars advocating decolonisation focus on both the epistemic and material aspects of decolonisation, there is a tendency in scholarship to focus one's attention on one over the other. This points back to assumptions about the core mechanism of oppression in development. Is it knowledge and discourse, culminating in the GN's power over the Global South (GS) through framing and representation of the GS? Alternatively, is the core mechanism of oppression the material power of the GN over the GS? This material power of the GN includes structural power, especially within the international political economy, and the constraints that the GN puts on development in the GS, through transnational corporations, international financial institutions, global finance, trade, and investment.

An understanding of decolonisation requires engagement with both the intellectual and material aspects of oppression. Development Studies needs to pursue intellectual decolonisation, defined as centring GS scholars and theory and thus the pluralisation of knowledge beyond Anglo-Saxon scholars, while also remaining robust in its critique of the material political economy dimensions of contemporary imperialism and hierarchy in a GN-dominated global economy that constrains the development of GS. However, this framing of 'pluralisation' retains parameters on what constitutes scientific knowledge.

The case that decolonisation should be approached largely as a discursive/epistemic question, as discussed, emanates from Said's critique of representation. Foucault's discursive power and Bourdieu's symbolic power are also evident. Escobar's (1992; 1995) original critique of development that launched post-development theory was based on such notions of power as discursive and internalised. Specifically, Development Studies had a neo-colonial agenda of imposing a Western agenda of superiority and the superiority of modernity on 'the Other', meaning the GS. This original critique fell somewhat from prominence for several reasons. Some say it was nihilistic, romanticising the traditional, and was effectively pulling away the ladder from the GS by rejecting 'development' or modernity as an idea (see Kiely, 1999; Pailey, 2020).

Over the last decade or two, decolonial theory in Development Studies has become much more evident. In particular, this has been driven by the 'decolonial turn' (Grosfoguel, 2007) or 'race and decolonial turn' (Patel, 2020) in social sciences. It is argued that Development Studies ignores racial hierarchies and has what Pailey (2020) calls the 'white gaze'. Further, Development Studies is considered part of the 'geopolitics' of knowledge, and its production and use, meaning knowledge produced in the GN, by GN scholars, about the GS (see for a range of discussion, Kothari et al., 2019; Mignolo, 2021; Pailey, 2020; Patel, 2020).

Race is an important part of this. Quijano (2000) in a core concept of decolonial thought refers to the 'colonial matrix of power' meaning, racial/cultural classification based on whiteness as superior, the control of labour and resources, the domination of European ways of knowing, and the hierarchies created by colonisation and neo-colonisation. In a similar vein, Castro-Gómez (2007) refers to the triangular structure of coloniality: the coloniality of being, the coloniality of power, and the coloniality of knowledge. In short, coloniality is expressed by racism and a system of oppression sustained by capitalism, patriarchy, human/nature dissociation, and linguistic supremacy among other components.

In short, this is an epistemic/discursive perspective on power in several ways. First, decolonisation is beyond material reality, meaning the basis of power is discursive/epistemic. Second, discursive/epistemic decolonisation is also about race, racial hierarchy, and 'the white gaze' of knowledge about the GS produced by GN scholars. Third, epistemic decolonisation entails a rejection of Western modernity as desirable development. Fourth, and crucial for Development Studies, discursive/epistemic decolonisation concerns the relations of knowledge production. Next, we consider each.

First, there is the component that discursive/epistemic decolonisation is beyond the political process of material decolonisation or struggle against imperial powers that began in the early 1900s in Africa or 200 years ago in Latin America, entailing political and economic independence from colonisers. Scholars of epistemic decolonisation argue that decolonisation cannot be reduced to material colonialism or neo-colonialism of economic and political matters. Instead, according to Ndlovu-Gatsheni (2020, p. 94):

> The modern world system is an epistemic creation, and its shifting global orders are epistemic creations. By the same logic, what exists as economy, society, and politics are all epistemic creations. What is termed "development" is also an epistemic creation.

Colonisation, in the words of Grosfoguel (2002, p. 220), is about the

> ... cultural, political, sexual, spiritual, epistemic, and economic oppression/exploitation of subordinate racialized/ethnic groups by dominant racialized/ethnic groups with or without the existence of colonial administrations.

Second, following on from this point is that discursive/epistemic decolonisation is about race and specifically, 'whiteness', meaning the subjectification or the attempt to 'turn the colonised into less than human beings' (Lugones, 2010, p. 745). This is done by creating a sense of 'whiteness as superior and synonymous with civilisation', thus legitimising a hierarchy of race (Ndlovu-Gatsheni, 2013, p. 31). In sum, the argument, resonating with Said, is that colonialism legitimised racial hierarchies, which continue today. Thus, domination entails racial attributes of the 'uncivilised' and 'underdeveloped' countries and people. A racial hierarchy defines which countries are developed or underdeveloped (Marchand and Parpart, 1995). Thus, the aid and development industry are historical continuities to 'civilise' the GS.

Quijano (2000) too focuses on the power of classification. Resonating with Foucault, they argue that classification is racist and that racial hierarchies exist within the worldview of Eurocentric modernity. With reference to race, it is also argued that there is a need to avoid 'whitening' the term 'decolonise' by depoliticising it, as is the case in Western universities, where the term has become a buzzword for equality initiatives that may be tokenistic (Behari-Leak, 2019; Moosavi, 2020).

Third, discursive/epistemic decolonisation entails a partial or perhaps outright rejection of Western modernity, specifically what Sondarjee and Andrews (2023, p. 7) call 'the colonial blueprint' for what is considered to be a modern society. Indeed, the argument is made that the liberation movements of the 1950s/1960s failed because they chose to emulate Western efforts to 'modernise' and discipline 'uncivilised' societies in keeping with a Western notion of progress (Rutazibwa, 2018). Maldonado-Torres (2011) goes a step further to argue that there is a 'family' of thought cohering around modernity as the core development problem. Concurring with Mignolo (2011), they posit that a 'de-linking (epistemically and politically) from the web of imperial knowledge' is required. Mignolo's (2007, p. 453) earlier work developed this 'delinking' concept as 'a de-colonial epistemic shift leading to "other-universality", that is, to "pluri-versality" as a universal project'. However, delinking may presuppose relinking. This could be manifest in 'the recovery of knowledge(s) and praxes that have been historically omitted from the major global agendas, as well as in the circulation of dissident "glocal" narratives that question the meta-narrative of development and capitalism' according to Garcia-Arias and Cuestas-Caza (2024, p. 8). All claims to knowledge could potentially be counted as knowledge within this perspective without any hierarchy of scientific or non-scientific criteria. Epistemic delinking is then a delinking from colonial 'mindsets' so that other epistemologies, other principles of knowledge and understanding and, consequently, other economics, other politics, and other ethics may emerge unhindered by suppression. The concept of the 'pluriversality' is central and oft cited as required, rejecting any hierarchy of knowledge or thought, leading to 'a world in which many worlds exist un-hierarchised' (Ndlovu-Gatsheni, 2020, p. 39). The risk in such approach is that the importance of knowledge on material imperialism is negated amid the expansion of knowledge without limits of scientific criteria.

Finally, discursive/epistemic decolonisation also concerns the relations of knowledge production, which is important to Development Studies as an endeavour of knowledge production. The analogy of relations of production entails an 'elite' and a 'working class' or a set of 'elite' scholars in the GN who dominate what gets researched and how and 'working class' scholars in the GS that may do much of the data collection.

This discussion is of direct relevance to Development Studies. As any knowledge endeavour, in principle it has the power to silence voices from the GS by the dominance of Northern-based universities, funding, journals, and so forth. There are two points: (i) the tension between 'scientific' and other forms of knowledge such as Indigenous knowledge and that decolonisation requires 're-centring' of marginalised knowledges; (ii) the issue of languages, colonial languages, being imposed on the colonised and functioning as a means of controlling ways of thinking and seeing the world, also referred to as 'epistemicides' and 'linguisticides', respectively, the destruction of Indigenous worldviews and languages (de Jong et al., 2018; de Sousa Santos, 2014; Smith, 1999). From a discursive/epistemic view, decolonisation means to 'value, make visible, and amplify Global South voices rather than co-opting their intellectual production', thus freeing the 'captive mind' (Alatas, 1974, p. 698).

If we turn to a materialist approach to power and politics, we see a very different approach. Nassen Smith and Lester (2023), for example, make a set of arguments from a material political economy perspective, drawing on the thinking of Samir Amin. The authors look back to identify the cultural turn in social sciences and social theory in the 1970s (as discussed in Chapter 2). Specifically, how social theory shifted from economic determinism to cultural determinism, leading to forms of relativism that elevated culture in theories of social reality and social life. The authors contend that epistemic/discursive decolonisation approaches suffer from a too strong tendency towards culturalism, idealism, and relativism. They disagree that persistent domination of the GN over the GS is due to Eurocentric forms of knowledge and epistemology. They argue that this is misdirected, resonating with Amin (1989; see also

2010) and Wallerstein (1997), who contest the idea of a uniform 'Western culture', and holds that structural political-economy relations and not culture or knowledge alone are primary in explaining domination, against the culturalist emphasis associated with readings of Said (1978; 1983; 1993). Hence, knowledge and culture are not the primary pathway of oppression. They posit that cultural-based theories take for granted what needs to be explained (i.e., the systems of domination) and distract from the primary causes of underdevelopment in the form of moral relativism.

In sum, epistemic and discursive de/colonisation directly confronts the colonisation of knowledge, aiming to rebuild and legitimise non-Western forms of knowledge while recognising all sources of knowledge and examining non-Western knowledge systems to rectify the epistemic injustices of colonialism. Material decolonisation, however, pertains to the physical aspects of decolonisation, such as ensuring economic justice and political sovereignty for Global South countries. While epistemic decolonisation addresses knowledge systems and paradigms, material decolonisation concentrates on tangible elements, such as economic hierarchies in the global economy and international governance. The notions of power and politics are fundamentally different.

5.4.1 Decolonisation and Development Studies: Of What and How?

What does the preceding discussion imply for Development Studies itself? Kapoor (2023) provides a survey of debates and asserts that to foster a more inclusive, equitable, and just approach, Development Studies needs to integrate epistemic and material decolonisation strategies by confronting the tendencies within Development Studies towards amnesia, which erases the history and impacts of European colonialism. Development Studies can challenge Eurocentric pedagogies, Kapoor argues, by promoting equitable partnerships in research and resisting neo-colonial practices such as who decides what to research. In other words, critically engaging with historical power dynamics and embracing more diverse knowledge production systems.

Kapoor thus proposes intertwining intellectual and material decolonisation. The intellectual approach entails expanding and 'democratising' Development Studies by retrieving non-Western and subaltern/Indigenous texts, writers, and practices. The aim is to make the curriculum more inclusive and interdisciplinary, not just to sanction non-Western knowledge but to broaden the range of voices that count as knowledge within Development Studies. However, this approach also poses challenges because there is a risk of replacing old power inequalities with new ones because of the need to determine who defines the boundaries of robust knowledge. Intellectual decolonisation could inadvertently perpetuate new forms of power inequality, as Kapoor notes, if there are selective readings and interpretations of history.

Taylor et al. (2024) present a set of reflections on decolonising knowledge (see also Taylor and Tremblay, 2022). The authors focus on four questions. Specifically, what, and whose, knowledge is valued, counted, and integrated into development processes? How do researchers/educators go about decolonising knowledge asymmetries, learning through research and teaching? What kinds of investment are needed to promote learning and change? And what is researchers'/educators' role in transformations, as individuals, as organisations, as institutions? On the first question (whose knowledge is valued), they stress the need to recognise Indigenous and local knowledge systems. On the second question, they suggest that researchers/educators in Development Studies should reflect on research practices and partnerships and seek to address power imbalances. On the third question, they call for investments in patience, humility, and financial resources. Finally, on the fourth question, they emphasise the responsibility of individuals and organisations to commit to intellectual decolonisation.

The question of the power dynamics in research relationships is also important. To this end, Ordóñez Llanos et al. (2024) discuss the complexities in promoting equitable relationships across GN-GS research. They note that while Northern funders and institutions promote the idea of equitable partnerships, it is often given insufficient prioritisation. Speaking to a range of stakeholders, they found that there is a lack of a common way of seeing equity. Underlying this is a sense from GS researchers that there is low recognition of research that originates in the GS and a limited role in setting discussions about knowledge as well as competing incentives. Researchers in the GN, on the other hand, feel limited by risk management processes, an overreliance on project-based funding, and metrics of research excellence. Points of convergence include acknowledgement of the power imbalances between GN and GS researchers and a strong and growing sense that needs addressing. Ultimately, there is the issue of agency (or lack of it) of GS scholars in determining what gets funded, what gets researched, and what gets published. They argue that rather than seeking ways of GS scholars answering research questions set by GN scholars or GS scholars collecting data only for GN scholars to publish it, there is a need to set the research agenda in an equitable way from start to finish.

Rather than focusing solely on material or intellectual decolonisation, Development Studies needs to address the continuing impacts of (neo)colonialism on knowledge production. It must also address socio-economic structures and hierarchies. Epistemic efforts alone are insufficient without material decolonisation and vice versa. Kapoor's proposition of intertwining these strategies entails confronting historical power dynamics and promoting equitable research partnerships to foster a more just knowledge production system which would strive to address knowledge asymmetries and power imbalances. This entails deeper thought about whose knowledge is valued, promoting investments in equitable research practices, and committing to the transformative responsibilities of individuals and institutions. Ultimately, the entire discussion is about the need for Development Studies to aim for deeper engagement with the power dynamics of research relationships, avoiding 'extractive' research. Equitable partnerships between Global North and Global South researchers require genuine recognition of Southern scholarship and collaborative agenda-setting from inception to publication.

5.5 Conclusions

In conclusion, this chapter has sought to underscore the importance of reflecting on the ontological and epistemological aspects of development and its study and, in particular, how disciplines approach power and politics differently. Given the quite different ways in which power and politics are conceptualised across disciplines, this reflection is particularly important to Development Studies. Further, following from this point is an argument that decolonisation encompasses both intellectual and material dimensions.

Abstract ideas of the onto-epistemology of development flow through to framing core concepts of power and politics. Thus, they ultimately lead to different ways to characterise and theorise about the mechanisms of power and politics. This chapter has argued that it is important not to overlook the interplay and trade-offs between conceptualising decolonisation primarily as either a material or intellectual concern. The debate surrounding decolonisation in Development Studies has gained significant traction in recent years, driven by the recognition of the enduring impacts of colonialism and the need to dismantle entrenched systems of oppression. At the heart of this lie two questions: How should Development Studies respond to the decolonisation critique? And to what extent should it prioritise epistemic or material decolonisation? This chapter has explored these questions in terms of elevating the voices and knowledge production of the Global South (epistemic decolonisation) and addressing the structural inequalities perpetuated by the global political economy (material decolonisation).

Although the call to prioritise epistemic decolonisation is pervasive and advocates for a reconfiguration of power dynamics in knowledge production, challenging the dominance of Western-focused perspectives, and amplifying the voices of the GS, the importance of material decolonisation should not be underestimated. Structural disparities stemming from centuries of colonial and neo-colonial exploitation and imperialism continue.

6
Conclusion

Development and its Discontents. Andy Sumner, Oxford University Press. © Andy Sumner (2026).
DOI: 10.1093/9780198902904.003.0006

6.1 Introduction

This concluding chapter returns to the starting point of the book. The international context is increasingly uncertain, marked by geopolitical tensions, fractured multilateralism, and deepening global inequalities. These conditions shape how development is understood, theorised, and contested. Assumptions from the post–Cold War era included liberal globalisation, rising multilateral cooperation, and steady progress in prosperity for many countries. These are now unsettled by a confluence of crises, from climate shocks and pandemics to political polarisation and economic volatility. For Development Studies, the challenge is to respond to the disarray and also to reflect on the nature of its own intellectual endeavour. The book itself has argued that the field finds itself is increasingly pluralised, with diverse and sometimes incompatible modes of thought. This concluding chapter brings together the central threads of the book and reflects on the current intellectual condition of Development Studies.

As outlined in Chapter 1, DS today occupies a paradoxical space: it is simultaneously thriving and fragmenting. The field enjoys significant institutional robustness in terms of teaching programmes, vibrant scholarly associations, departments and institutes, and an ever growing volume of research output. Yet, beneath this institutional health lies persistent and possibly intensifying internal divergences, a divergence of worldviews and modes of thought. This book describes signs of a potential 'new impasse' in Development Studies. It is not a replay of the 1980s/1990s impasse, but a proliferation of epistemic and conceptual divides. These divides limit the field's coherence and may constrain scope for genuine interdisciplinarity.

This book sought to interrogate these issues by presenting a mapping of Development Studies across three continua, framing, scope, and onto-epistemology. These were not intended as definitive or exhaustive but rather as heuristics to help clarify where and how intellectual divergences manifest within Development Studies. More importantly, the book has argued that these divergences matter, not because consensus must be imposed, but because understanding the nature of disagreement is a precondition for exchanges and more meaningful interdisciplinarity. In short, Development Studies is a field defined less by agreement on core concepts, theories, or methods, and more by a set of recurring questions that different schools answer in fundamentally different ways.

This concluding chapter is structured as follows. Section 2 revisits the intellectual context for the book and re-engages with the idea of a potential new impasse in DS. Section 3 synthesises the key arguments presented across the three continua, framing, scope, and onto-epistemology. Section 4 turns to the question of intellectual renewal, outlining proposals to facilitate more productive engagement across modes of thought with the goal of facilitating deeper interdisciplinarity. Section 5 offers closing reflections on the future of DS with some scenarios.

6.2 Development Studies and the New Impasse?

As discussed in Chapter 1, the origins of DS are entwined with both imperialism and anti-imperialism, reflecting a dialectic that has shaped the field since its inception. DS emerged as a cross-disciplinary project rooted in the post-war and post-colonial reordering of the world. Its institutional foundations were laid by scholars working in institutions shaped by Cold War logics. The field was marked early on by a tension between technocratic approaches to poverty alleviation and transformative visions of national economic development. These foundational tensions have never been fully resolved. Instead, they have multiplied.

The 'impasse' debates of the 1980s and 1990s (e.g., Munck and O'Hearn, 1999; Schuurman, 1993), as noted in Chapter 1, marked a critical moment in which DS faced deep epistemological and normative disillusionment. Post-structuralist critiques challenged the foundational assumption of development theory, namely the desirability of modernity, and questioned the very idea of development as a universal telos. Development theory, while analytically powerful, came under scrutiny for determinism and the sense of limited agency for the GS. The result was not a collapse of the field but a fragmentation towards epistemic pluralism and disagreements on common reference points.

This book has argued that there is a potential for a comparable new impasse. This is not a crisis, but the cumulative effect of intellectual differentiation. Today, DS is characterised by multiple, co-existing 'modes of thought', each with its own conceptual vocabulary, preferred methods, and divergent theories on what are the core mechanisms of power and oppression. These modes are not merely academic preferences; they embody different understandings of what development is, who it is for, and how it should be studied. While this diversity is often celebrated, it also raises difficult questions about the coherence of the field and the limits on greater interdisciplinarity.

6.3 Framing, Scope, and Onto-Epistemology across the Modes of Thought

This book has examined the diversity of Development Studies through three continua, which function as analytical tools to trace divergence across the field. Each continuum speaks to a fundamental question in DS, and each reveals fault lines between the major schools of thought in Development Studies.

The framing continuum addresses the question: What kind of change does development entail? Is it about transformation, radical, systemic, and structural, or is it about fixing and improving existing institutions and systems? Chapter 3 noted how different schools of thought diverge in their orientation towards transformation. Classical Development Studies, influenced by structuralism and early development economics, has favoured major transformative change, understood in terms of industrialisation and national economic sovereignty. Post-development and decolonial approaches also call for transformation, though of a different kind: not economic modernisation but a rejection or reconfiguration of parts or all of modernity itself and what is to be valued and thus pursued. By contrast, Problem-Solving Development Studies, aligned with policy-oriented and technocratic approaches, tends to adopt a reformist stance, emphasising governance, service delivery, and poverty alleviation. Global Development Studies somewhat straddles both sides, combining systemic aspirations with technocratic implementation. These divergences reflect fundamentally different understandings of what counts as Chambers (2004) 'good change' and, implicitly, of what the purpose of DS should be.

The scope continuum asks: Where does development occur, and to whom does it apply? Is development a universal process relevant to all countries, or is it specific to a certain group of countries, namely the Global South? Chapter 4 revisited the long-standing binary of North and South and asked whether the differentiation remains analytically and politically salient. Global Development Studies challenges the GN/GS binary, arguing that issues such as inequality, environmental degradation, and political crisis are global in scope and across GN and GS. However, it was argued that this position risks overlooking the structural asymmetries that continue to define the global political economy.

The book argued that despite economic growth in parts of the Global South, deep-rooted differences in structural characteristics, institutional constraints, and historical legacies persist. Ignoring these differences risks erasing the specific challenges faced by GS or 'late' developing countries. Hence, while the GN/GS binary may be imperfect, abandoning it altogether is both analytically and normatively premature, it was argued. Instead, a trinary is re-emerging, echoing Wallerstein (1974a; 1974b; 1976).

The third continuum, the onto-epistemological, asks: What is the nature of social reality, and how can it be known in Development Studies? This is perhaps the most abstract of the three continua, but also the most profound in shaping the practice and politics of DS. Chapter 5 examined how different schools of thought in DS draw on competing epistemological traditions: positivism, realism, and relativism. These underpin divergent views on politics and power, the relationship between knowledge and power, the role of objectivity/subjectivity in research, and the nature of what counts as evidence. For example, positivist traditions emphasise observable, measurable data and tend to be evident in economics-leaning approaches. Realist traditions accept an independent reality but highlight the limits of observation. Relativist or constructivist traditions reject the idea of universal truth, focusing instead on meaning, discourse, and positionality and are clearly evident in post-development/decolonial thought. Each of these onto-epistemological positions also implies quite different or incommensurate understandings of power and the mechanisms of politics. For some, power is material, grounded in political economy structures. For others, it is epistemic, embedded in discourses that produce subjects and hierarchies of knowledge with real-world consequences. Still others see power as institutional, shaped by rules and norms. These differing perspectives and others beyond these generate divergent strategies for any kind of development.

6.4 Intellectual Renewal

As argued in this book, Development Studies is defined by co-existing modes of thought that differ across the continua of framing, scope, and onto-epistemology. The task is to decide whether, and how, dialogue across these divides can be cultivated to achieve deeper interdisciplinarity. Intellectual pluralism is not inherently a bad thing. Indeed, it has long been a source of creativity and contestation in Development Studies. It has enabled the field to evolve in response to shifting global conditions in the past as well as critiques from within. But the present moment suggests a tipping point: the risk is not pluralism per se, but unacknowledged or deepening differentiation that hardens into siloed thinking, or echo chambers. The goal of this book was never a dialogue leading to a consensus that could be found to some extent in constituent social science disciplines (especially on core concepts and methodologies). Nor was the aim to smooth over real and meaningful differences. Rather, the aim is to create the conditions under which disagreement can be productive rather than separating and thus to enable scholars, practitioners, and students to engage across boundaries with respect and thoughtfulness. The continua map difference. This section now proposes tentative bridges across those divides. The four proposals below are neither exhaustive nor prescriptive. They are invitations to reimagine how Development Studies might become more experimental, reflective, outward-looking, and ultimately more interdisciplinary.

6.4.1 Decentring 'Development' as the Core Organising Concept

One of the most persistent challenges in DS is the contested nature of the very concept it is named after. For students encountering DS for the first time, the ambiguity of 'development' can be both intriguing and confusing. The word 'development' has become a flashpoint term, invested with multiple and often conflicting meanings. For some, it continues to signify an aspirational project of economic and social transformation in the Global South. For others, it is an emblem of neo-colonialism, epistemic domination, and technocratic interventionism. This dissonance is not merely semantic. It reflects divergent normative orientations and ontological assumptions about what societies are, how they change, and what counts as progress. Attempts to reconcile these meanings often fall short. Instead, a more generative approach might lie in decentring 'development' itself as the core organising concept of the field. This does not entail abandoning the concept entirely. Rather, it suggests a move towards foregrounding adjacent or alternative terms that may carry less historical and epistemic baggage while opening space for new discussions. Concepts such as inequality, or justice or emancipation, may provide for more inclusive and less polarising dialogue. These terms shift the focus from teleological narratives of progress to questions of power, distribution, and sustainability, and issues that are shared across multiple modes and schools of thought even if they are differently interpreted.

6.4.2 Experimenting with Ontological and Epistemological Flexibility

A second route towards intellectual renewal lies in cultivating greater openness to ontological and epistemological experimentation. As Chapter 5 argued, the different modes and schools of thought in Development Studies are underpinned by distinct assumptions about the nature of social reality and the means by which it can be known. These assumptions are deeply embedded in disciplinary training, methodological norms, and institutional structures. While such foundations are not inherently problematic, they can become constraining when treated as doctrinal. For example, positivist approaches tend to prioritise deductive reasoning, empirical verification, and generalisability, often favouring economics-leaning analysis. Relativist or constructivist approaches, by contrast, emphasise situated knowledge, reflexivity, and discursive analysis, more common in anthropology. Realist traditions occupy an intermediate position, seeking to reconcile structure and agency, objectivity and contingency. Each of these frameworks offers useful insights. However, when they become mutually exclusive, they limit the potential for collaboration or conceptual innovation. To move beyond this, DS scholars could loosen epistemic boundaries without abandoning rigour. They could engage in methodological and conceptual innovation, including greater use of mixed methods and cross-traditions theorising. They should also investigate the history of ideas and their Western and non-Western genealogies. Experimentation though requires some humility in the sense of an awareness of the partiality of all knowledge claims and a willingness to learn across perspectives. It is uncomfortable for any scholar.

6.4.3 Investing in Foundational Research

The third proposal concerns the need for renewed attention to foundational, meta-theoretical questions in DS. These include inquiries into the categories used, the assumptions inherited, and the frameworks deployed to understand social change. These are not questions that any one school or mode of thought could answer alone. They require collaboration across traditions and disciplines. A renewed emphasis on foundational research, that is, research that interrogates the epistemic, normative, and historical premises of Development Studies itself, can serve as a space of engagement between competing perspectives. Foundational research would be useful to re-ground the field in a common vocabulary even if it is contested to some extent.

6.4.4 Engaging More Deeply with Neighbouring Fields

A final strategy for intellectual renewal is to expand the horizon of DS by engaging more deliberately with neighbouring fields. Area Studies and International Studies, in particular, offer useful points of connection. Both are cross-disciplinary, and both in their social turn, concerned with power and politics. Yet they approach these questions through different epistemic traditions and regional lenses, often privileging context over abstraction. Area Studies, with its emphasis on linguistic and cultural fluency, provides deep empirical grounding that can complement DS. It reminds DS scholars that categories like 'state', 'market', or 'civil society' apply unevenly across contexts. And that development cannot be understood without attention to historical and cultural specificity. International Studies brings a focus on global structures of governance, sovereignty, and conflict with a social turn. Although IR has traditionally centred state actors and security paradigms, critical currents within the field are increasingly attuned to questions of inequality, resistance, and global justice, making them fertile ground for dialogue with DS. Other adjacent fields, such as political ecology, global sociology, and critical global health, also offer conceptual and methodological innovations. These conversations may help Development Studies navigate the challenge of maintaining its normative orientation in its commitment to justice, equity, and emancipation without becoming intellectually insular.

In sum, these proposals, decentring 'development', experimenting, renewing foundational research, and engaging neighbouring fields, are offered as provocations. They reflect a belief that the future of DS depends not on consensus, but on the capacity to speak across difference.

6.5 Conclusion

Development Studies is not in decline, nor is it in a state of crisis currently. The field remains vibrant in terms of research output, institutional presence, and teaching programmes. But it also finds itself confronting a growing pluralism that may turn into greater internal conflict. The proliferation of divergent perspectives, while intellectually enriching, increasingly challenges the coherence of Development Studies as a shared space of inquiry.

This book has argued that contemporary Development Studies is shaped by the continua of framing, scope, and onto-epistemology. These provide a structured way to understand how and why different schools of thought within the field arrive at different conclusions about what development is, where it happens, and how it should be studied. In mapping these divergences, the book has not sought to seek resolution. Rather, it has aimed to make disagreement clearer and, therefore, more open to engagement.

Unlike the earlier impasse of the 1980s and 1990s, which was driven by theoretical exhaustion and the perceived failures of grand narratives, today's potential impasse is different. There is no shortage of ideas, theories, or critiques. But there is a lack of shared frameworks through which these can productively interact. Without such frameworks, the risk is that Development Studies becomes that set of echo chambers.

Of course, the future of Development Studies will not be determined solely by intellectual debates. Institutional, political, and generational shifts will shape the field as much as any other drivers. Nevertheless, the way Development Studies confronts its internal tensions will have implications for its credibility, and coherence in the decades to come.

What might those futures look like? Three broad scenarios could be imagined: First, continuation of fragmentation. One possible future is that the current trajectory continues. Schools of thought become increasingly siloed, cross-school, interdisciplinary dialogue declines, and scholars retreat into their own familiar paradigms. The field remains active but increasingly compartmentalised, with limited collaboration across divides. This may not lead to collapse, but it risks stasis or an inability to respond creatively to new global challenges or to engage with emerging perspectives.

Second, the emergence of dominant paradigm in DS that is hegemonic in the Kuhnian sense. This means a dominant paradigm that reorganises the field around a new orthodoxy, perhaps through a dominant methodological approach. While this might restore a degree of coherence, it would come at the cost of diversity. Heterodox or critical perspectives could be marginalised. DS would regain unity, but potentially at the expense of reflexivity and plurality.

Third, constructive pluralism. The most hopeful future, albeit the most demanding. This is where pluralism is a source of intellectual vitality. In this future, scholars engage more openly across schools or modes of thought to situate their own positions and understand others. Dialogue is not about agreement, but about mutual intelligibility and shared inquiry. In this scenario, new research questions emerge that cut across established ways of working. Methodological innovation flourishes as does interdisciplinarity and researchers experiment with hybrid designs, mixed methods and perhaps even mixed-epistemologies, and co-produce knowledge. Pedagogically, students are trained not just in content, but in how to navigate intellectual diversity.

The final note of this book is not that Development Studies should eliminate its internal tensions. That was never the intention of the book. Instead, researchers should travel across borders, and work at their edges as difficult as that may be. Scholars could inhabit the overlaps between views and to create conceptual vocabularies that allow ideas to travel. Some scholars already operate at the junction points between different schools and many scholars move schools over their career, having a foot in more than one camp so this is not necessarily unusual for some. In doing so, Development Studies might be better equipped for the future.

References

Abbott, A. (2002). 'The disciplines and the future', in Brint, S. (ed.) The Future of the City of Intellect: The Changing American University. Stanford, CA: Stanford University Press.

Acemoglu, D. and Robinson, J. A. (2012). Why Nations Fail: The Origins of Power, Prosperity, and Poverty. New York: Crown Business.

Acosta, A. (2013). 'Extractivism and neoextractivism: Two sides of the same curse', in Lang, M. and Mokrani, D. (eds) Beyond Development: Alternative Visions from Latin America. Amsterdam/Quito: Rosa Luxemburg Stiftung and Transnational Institute, pp. 61–86.

Adom, P. K. (2024). The Socioeconomic Impact of Climate Change in Developing Countries in the Next Decades: A Review. CGD Working Paper 681. Washington, DC: Center for Global Development.

Alatas, S. H. (1974). The Captive Mind and Creative Development. International Social Science Journal, 26(4), 691–700.

Alemany, C., Slatter, C., and Rodríguez Enríquez, C. (2019). Gender Blindness and the Annulment of the Development Contract. Development and Change, 50(2), 468–483.

Alvares, C. (1992). Science, Development and Violence: The Revolt against Modernity. Delhi/New York: Oxford University Press.

Amin, S. (1974). Accumulation on a World Scale: A Critique of the Theory of Underdevelopment. New York: Monthly Review Press.

Amin, S. (1976). Unequal Development: An Essay on the Social Formations of Peripheral Capitalism. New York: Monthly Review Press.

Amin, S. (1977). Imperialism and Unequal Development. New York: Monthly Review Press.

Amin, S. (1980). Class and Nation, Historically and in the Current Crisis. New York: Monthly Review Press.

Amin, S. (1989). Eurocentrism. New York: Monthly Review Press.

Amin, S. (1990). Delinking: Towards a Polycentric World. London: Zed Books.

Amin, S. (1997). Capitalism in the Age of Globalization: The Management of Contemporary Society. London: Zed Books.

Amin, S. (2010). Global History: A View from the South. Oxford: Pambazuka Press.

Ayer, A. J. (1936). Language, Truth and Logic. London: Victor Gollancz.

Bangura, Y. (2019). Convergence Is Not Equality. Development and Change, 50(2), 394–409.

Battiste, M. and Henderson, J. Y. (2000). Protecting Indigenous Knowledge and Heritage: A Global Challenge. Vancouver: UBC Press.

Baud, I., Basile, E., Kontinen, T., and von Itter, S. (eds.) (2019). Building Development Studies for the New Millennium. Cham: Palgrave Macmillan.

Baymul, C. and Sen, K. (2020). Was Kuznets Right? New Evidence on the Relationship between Structural Transformation and Inequality. The Journal of Development Studies, 56(9), 1643–1662.

Behari-Leak, K. (2019). Decolonial Turns, Postcolonial Shifts, and Cultural Connections: Are We There Yet?. English Academy Review, 36(1), 58–68.

Behuria, P. (2025). Is the Study of Development Humiliating or Emancipatory? The Case against Universalising "Development". The European Journal of Development Research, 37(2), 344–355.

Bergstrøm, C. and Molteberg, E. (2000). Our Common Discourse: Diversity and Paradigms in Development Studies (Paper No. 2 of 2). NORAGRIC Working Paper No. 21. Ås: Agricultural University of Norway, NORAGRIC.

Bermeo, S. B. (2018). Targeted Development: Industrialized Country Strategy in a Globalizing World. New York: Oxford University Press.
Bernstein, H. (2005). 'Development studies and the Marxists', in Kothari, U. (ed.) A Radical History of Development Studies: Individuals, Institutions and Ideologies. London: Zed Books, 111–137.
Bevan, P. (2003). Extending Understanding of Chronic Poverty Dynamics: Towards a Post-Disciplinary Approach. Conference paper presented at "Staying Poor: Chronic Poverty and Development Policy", University of Manchester, 7–9 April 2003. Chronic Poverty Research Centre.
Bevan, P. (2004a). Studying Poverty and Inequality in Poor Countries: Getting to Grips with Structure. University of Bath, Department of Economics and International Development.
Bevan, P. (2004b). Exploring the Structured Dynamics of Chronic Poverty: A Sociological Approach. WeD Working Paper 6. Bath: University of Bath, Wellbeing in Developing Countries (WeD) Research Centre.
Bevan, P. (2005). Studying Multi-Dimensional Poverty in Ethiopia: Towards a Q-Integrated Approach. Q-Squared Working Paper No. 15. University of Toronto, Centre for International Studies.
Bevan, P. (2007). 'Researching wellbeing across the disciplines: Some key intellectual problems and ways forward', in Gough, I. and McGregor, J. A. (eds.) Well-Being in Developing Countries: From Theory to Research. Cambridge: Cambridge University Press, 283–315.
Bhambra, G. K. (2014). Postcolonial and Decolonial Dialogues. Postcolonial Studies, 17(2), 115–121.
Bhaskar, R. (1979). The Possibility of Naturalism: A Philosophical Critique of the Contemporary Human Sciences. Brighton: Harvester Press.
Bizhan, N. (ed.) (2022). State Fragility: Case Studies and Comparisons. London: Routledge.
Blaikie, N. (1993). Approaches to Social Enquiry. Cambridge: Polity Press.
Booth, D. (1985). Marxism and Development Sociology: Interpreting the Impasse. World Development, 13(7), 761–787.
Bourdieu, P. (1984) Distinction: A Social Critique of the Judgement of Taste, trans. R. Nice. London: Routledge.
Bourdieu, P. (1986). 'The forms of capital', in Richardson, J. G. (ed.) Handbook of Theory and Research for the Sociology of Education (pp. 241–258). New York: Greenwood.
Bourdieu, P. (1989). Social Space and Symbolic Power. Sociological Theory, 7(1), 14–25.
Bourdieu, P. (1990). The Logic of Practice. Trans. R. Nice. Stanford, CA: Stanford University Press.
Bourdieu, P. and Wacquant, L. J. D. (1992). An Invitation to Reflexive Sociology. Chicago: University of Chicago Press.
Bresser-Pereira, L. C. (2011). From the National-Bourgeoisie to the Dependency Interpretation of Latin America. Latin American Perspectives, 38(3), 40–58.
Briggs, R. C. (2024). Beliefs, Values, and Practices in Development Studies. The Journal of Development Studies, 60(10), 1493–1510.
Büscher, B. (2019). From 'Global' to 'Revolutionary' Development. Development and Change, 50(2), 484–494.
de la Cadena, M. and Blaser, M. (eds.) (2018). A World of Many Worlds. Durham, NC: Duke University Press.
Cardoso, F. H. and Faletto, E. (1979). Dependency and Development in Latin America. Berkeley: University of California Press.
Carment, D. and Samy, Y. (eds.) (2023). Handbook of Fragile States. Cheltenham, UK: Edward Elgar Publishing.
Castro-Gómez, S. (2007). 'Decolonizar la universidad. La hybris del punto cero y el diálogo de saberes', in Castro-Gómez,S. and Grosfoguel, R. (eds.) El giro decolonial: Reflexiones para una diversidad epistémica más allá del capitalismo global (pp. 79–91). Bogotá: Siglo del Hombre Editores.

Césaire, A. (2000). Discourse on Colonialism. Trans. J. Pinkham. New York: Monthly Review Press.

Chambers, R. (1997). Whose Reality Counts? Putting the First Last. London: Intermediate Technology Publications.

Chambers, R. (2004). Ideas for Development: Reflecting Forwards. IDS Working Paper 238. Brighton: Institute of Development Studies.

Chambers, R. (2005). 'Critical reflections of a development nomad', in Kothari,U. (ed.) A Radical History of Development Studies: Individuals, Institutions and Ideologies (pp. 67–87). London: Zed Books.

Chambers, R. (2012). Provocations for Development. Rugby: Practical Action.

Chang, H.-J. (1994a). The Political Economy of Industrial Policy. Basingstoke and London: Macmillan.

Chang, H.-J. (1994b). State, Institutions, and Structural Change. Structural Change and Economic Dynamics, 5(2), 293–313.

Chang, H.-J. (2002). Breaking the Mould: An Institutionalist Political Economy Alternative to the Neo-Liberal Theory of the Market and the State. Cambridge Journal of Economics, 26(5), 539–559.

Chappell, R. Y. (2024). Why Not Effective Altruism?. Public Affairs Quarterly, 38(1), pp. 3–21.

Chimhowu, A. O., Hulme, D., and Munro, L. T. (2019). The 'New' National Development Planning and Global Development Goals: Processes and Partnerships. World Development, 120, 76–89.

Center for International Earth Science Information Network (CIESIN), Columbia University; CUNY Institute for Demographic Research (CIDR). (2021). Low Elevation Coastal Zone (LECZ) Urban-Rural Population and Land Area Estimates, Version 3 (1990, 2000, 2015) [dataset]. Palisades, NY: NASA SEDAC.

Connell, R. (2007). Southern Theory: The Global Dynamics of Knowledge in Social Science. Cambridge: Polity.

Cornwall, A. and Fujita, M. (2012). Ventriloquising "the Poor"? Of Voices, Choices and the Politics of "Participatory" Knowledge Production. Third World Quarterly, 33(9), 1751–1765.

Cowen, M. and Shenton, R. (1995). 'The invention of development', in Crush,J. (ed.) Power of Development. London/New York: Routledge.

Cowen, M. P. and Shenton, R. W. (1996). Doctrines of Development. London: Routledge.

Cox, R. W. (1981). Social Forces, States and World Orders: Beyond International Relations Theory. Millennium: Journal of International Studies, 10(2), 126–155.

Currie-Alder, B. (2016). The State of Development Studies: Origins, Evolution and Prospects. Canadian Journal of Development Studies, 37(1), 5–26.

Currie-Alder, B., Kanbur, R., Malone, D. M., and Medhora, R. (eds.) (2014). International Development: Ideas, Experience, and Prospects. Oxford: Oxford University Press.

Davies, T. R. (2024). World Order Transformation from the Grassroots: Global South Social Movements and the Transcendence of Established Approaches to International Change. International Political Sociology, 18(1), 1–24.

de Haan, A. and Maxwell, S. (1998). Editorial: Poverty and Social Exclusion in North and South. IDS Bulletin, 29(1), 1–9.

de Jong, S., Icaza, R., and Rutazibwa, O. U. (eds.) (2018). Decolonization and Feminisms in Global Teaching and Learning. Abingdon/New York: Routledge.

de Sousa Santos, B. (2007). Beyond Abyssal Thinking: From Global Lines to Ecologies of Knowledges. Review (Fernand Braudel Center), 30(1), 45–89.

de Sousa Santos, B. (2014). Epistemologies of the South: Justice against Epistemicide. Boulder, CO: Paradigm.

Deleuze, G. and Guattari, F. (1980). Mille plateaux. Paris: Minuit; English, 1987. A Thousand Plateaus: Capitalism and Schizophrenia. Trans. B. Massumi. Minneapolis: University of Minnesota Press.

Desai, V., and Potter, R. B. (eds.) (2014). The Companion to Development Studies (3rd ed.). London/New York: Routledge.

Dollar, D., and Kraay, A. (2002). Growth Is Good for the Poor. Journal of Economic Growth, 7(3), 195–225.
Dollar, D., Kleineberg, T., and Kraay, A. (2013). Growth Still Is Good for the Poor. Policy Research Working Paper No. 6568. Washington, DC: World Bank.
Dos Santos, T. (1970). The Structure of Dependence. American Economic Review, 60(2), 231–236.
Dow, S. C. (1990). Beyond Dualism. Cambridge Journal of Economics, 14(2), pp. 143–157.
Dow, S. C. (2002). Economic Methodology: An Inquiry. Oxford: Oxford University Press.
Dow, S. C. (2007). Variety of Methodological Approach in Economics. Journal of Economic Surveys, 21(3), pp. 447–465.
Dundas, P. (2002). The Jains (2nd ed.). London: Routledge.
Dussel, E. (2015). 'Modernidad y ethos barroco. Un diálogo con Bolívar Echeverría', in Filosofías del Sur. Descolonización y transmodernidad. Mexico City: Akal, pp. 295–317.
Echeverría, B. (1995). Las ilusiones de la modernidad. México, DF: UNAM/El Equilibrista.
Edwards, M. (1989). The Irrelevance of Development Studies. Third World Quarterly, 11(1), 116–135.
Eisenstadt, S.N. (2000). 'Multiple Modernities'. Daedalus, 129(1), 1–29.
Elman, B. A. (2005). On Their Own Terms: Science in China, 1550–1900. Cambridge, MA/London: Harvard University Press.
EM-DAT/CRED. (2024). 2023 Disasters in Numbers: A Significant Year of Disaster Impact. Brussels: Centre for Research on the Epidemiology of Disasters (UCLouvain, IRSS).
Escobar, A. (1992). Imagining a Post-Development Era? Critical Thought, Development and Social Movements. Social Text, (31/32), 20–56.
Escobar, A. (1995). Encountering Development: The Making and Unmaking of the Third World. Princeton, NJ: Princeton University Press.
Escobar, A. (2007). 'Post-development' as concept and social practice, in A. Ziai (ed.) Exploring Post-Development: Theory and Practice, Problems and Perspectives (pp. 18–31). London/New York: Routledge.
Esteva, G. (1985). Development: Metaphor, Myth, Threat. Development: Seeds of Change, 3, 78–79.
Esteva, G. (1992). 'Development', in Sachs,W. (ed.) The Development Dictionary: A Guide to Knowledge as Power (pp. 6–25). London: Zed Books.
Fanon, F. (1952). 'Peau noire, masques blancs. Paris: Éditions du Seuil', English: (1967) Black Skin, White Masks. Translated by C. L. Markmann. New York: Grove Press.
Fanon, F. (1961). Les Damnés de la Terre. Paris: François Maspero. English translations: (1963) The Wretched of the Earth, trans. Constance Farrington. New York: Grove Press.
Fanon, F. (1967). Toward the African Revolution: Political Essays, trans. Haakon Chevalier. New York: Grove Press, New York: Grove Press.
Felipe, J., Mehta, A. and Rhee, C. (2014). Manufacturing Matters ... but It's the Jobs That Count. ADB Economics Working Paper Series No. 420. Manila: Asian Development Bank.
Felipe, J., Mehta, A. and Rhee, C. (2019). Manufacturing Matters ... but It's the Jobs That Count. Cambridge Journal of Economics, 43(1): 139–168.
Ferguson, J. (1990). The Anti-Politics Machine: "Development", Depoliticization, and Bureaucratic Power in Lesotho. Cambridge: Cambridge University Press.
Feyerabend, P. (1975). Against Method: Outline of an Anarchistic Theory of Knowledge. London: New Left Books. (Later reprints by Verso).
Fine, B. (2002). Economics Imperialism and the New Development Economics as Kuhnian Paradigm Shift?. World Development, 30(12), 2057–2070.
Fischer, A. M. (2019). Bringing Development Back into Development Studies. Development and Change, 50(2), 426–444.
Foucault, M. (1970). The Order of Things: An Archaeology of the Human Sciences. New York: Pantheon Books; London: Tavistock Publications. [English translation by A. Sheridan of Les mots et les choses: Une archéologie des sciences humaines (1966)].

Foucault, M. (1972). The Archaeology of Knowledge. Translated by A. M. Sheridan Smith. New York: Pantheon; London: Tavistock. [English translation of *L'archéologie du savoir* (1969)].
Foucault, M. (1977). Discipline and Punish: The Birth of the Prison. London: Allen Lane. [English translation by A. Sheridan of Surveiller et punir: Naissance de la Prison (1975)].
Foucault, M. (1980). Power/Knowledge: Selected Interviews and Other Writings, 1972–1977. Edited by C. Gordon. Translated by C. Gordon, L. Marshall, J. Mepham and K. Soper. New York: Pantheon Books.
Foucault, M. (1991). "Governmentality", trans. R. Braidotti, in Burchell, G., Gordon, C., and Miller, P. (eds.) The Foucault Effect: Studies in Governmentality. Chicago: University of Chicago Press, pp. 87–104.
Fouré, J., Bénassy-Quéré, A., and Fontagné, L. (2012). The Great Shift: Macroeconomic Projections for the World Economy at the 2050 Horizon. CEPII Working Paper 2012-03. Paris: CEPII.
Frank, A. G. (1966). 'The development of underdevelopment', *Monthly Review*, 18(4), 17–31.
Frank, A. G. (1967). Capitalism and underdevelopment in Latin America: Historical studies of Chile and Brazil. New York: Monthly Review Press.
Fraser, C. (2014). Wandering the Way: A Eudaimonistic Approach to the Zhuangzi. Dao: A Journal of Comparative Philosophy, 13(4), pp. 541–565.
Fraser, C. (2024). Zhuangzi: Ways of Wandering the Way. Oxford: Oxford University Press.
Furtado, C. (1964). Development and Underdevelopment. Berkeley, CA: University of California Press.
Furtado, C. (1965). Development and Stagnation in Latin America: A Structuralist Approach. Studies in Comparative International Development, 1, pp. 159–175.
Gabuev, Alexander / Stuenkel, Oliver (2024): "The Battle for the BRICS. Why the Future of the Bloc Will Shape Global Order" in: *Foreign Affairs*, 24 September 2024: https://www.foreignaffairs.com/russia/battle-brics
Ganeri, J. (2011). The Lost Age of Reason: Philosophy in Early Modern India 1450–1700. Oxford: Oxford University Press.
García-Arias, J. and Cuestas-Caza, J. (2024). Pluriversal Autonomies Beyond Development.... Latin American Perspectives, 51(4), 122–140.
García-Arias, J., Tornel, C., and Flores Gutiérrez, M. (2025). Weaving a rhizomatic pluriverse.... Globalizations, 22(2), 302–322.
Gaventa, J. (1998). Poverty, Participation and Social Exclusion in North and South. IDS Bulletin, 29(1), 50–57.
George, R. A. (2025). Interdisciplinary, Multidisciplinary and Transdisciplinary Research: What's the Difference?. Bridging Boundaries: On Interdisciplinarity, Substack, 28 March. Available at: https://rachelageorge.substack.com/p/interdisciplinary-multidisciplinary (accessed 10 September 2025).
Gerschenkron, A. (1962). Economic Backwardness in Historical Perspective: A Book of Essays. Cambridge, MA: Belknap Press of Harvard University Press. (2015 reprint.)
Ghosh, J. (2019). A Brave New World, or the Same Old Story with New Characters? Development and Change, 50(2), 379–393.
Gills, B. K. and Hosseini, S. A. H. (2022). Pluriversality and Beyond: Consolidating Radical Alternatives to (Mal-)Development as a Commonist Project. Sustainability Science, 17(4), 1183–1194.
Gore, C. (2000). The Rise and Fall of the Washington Consensus as a Paradigm for Developing Countries. World Development, 28(5), 789–804.
Gradín, C. (2021). Trends in Global Inequality using a New Integrated Dataset. WIDER Working Paper 2021/61. Helsinki: UNU-WIDER.
Graeber, D. and Wengrow, D. (2021). The Dawn of Everything: A New History of Humanity. London: Allen Lane.

Griffel, F. (2007). 'Al-Ghazālī', in The Stanford Encyclopedia of Philosophy, edited by E. N. Zalta. Stanford, CA: Stanford University.
Griffel, F. (2009). Al-Ghazālī's Philosophical Theology. Oxford: Oxford University Press.
Grosfoguel, R. (2002). Colonial Difference, Geopolitics of Knowledge, and Global Coloniality in the Modern/Colonial Capitalist World-System. Review (Fernand Braudel Center), 25(3), pp. 203–224.
Grosfoguel, R. (2007). The Epistemic Decolonial Turn: Beyond Political-Economy Paradigms. Cultural Studies, 21(2–3), pp. 211–223.
Gudynas, E. (2011). Buen Vivir: Today's Tomorrow. Development, 54(4), pp. 441–447.
Gulliver, P. H. (1957). Interim Report on Land and Population in the Arusha Chiefdom. London: HMSO for the UK Colonial Office.
Gutas, D. (2014). Avicenna and the Aristotelian Tradition: Introduction to Reading Avicenna's Philosophical Works. 2nd rev. and enl. edn. Leiden/Boston: Brill.
Gyekye, K. (1995). *An Essay on African Philosophical Thought: The Akan Conceptual Scheme.* Revised edn. Philadelphia: Temple University Press.
Hall, P. A. and Taylor, R. C. R. (1996). Political Science and the Three New Institutionalisms. Political Studies, 44(5), pp. 936–957.
Harriss, J. (2002). Depoliticizing Development: The World Bank and Social Capital. London: Anthem Press.
Harriss, J. (2005). 'Great promise, hubris and recovery: A participant's history of development studies', in Kothari, U. (ed.) A Radical History of Development Studies: Individuals, Institutions and Ideologies. London: Zed Books, pp. 17–46.
Hart, G. (2001). Development Critiques in the 1990s: Culs De Sac and Promising Paths. Progress in Human Geography, 25(4), pp. 649–658.
Hart, G. (2002). Disabling Globalization: Places of Power in Post-Apartheid South Africa. Berkeley: University of California Press.
Hart, G. (2010). D/developments after the Meltdown. Antipode, 41(S1), 117–141.
Haug, S. (2021). A Thirdspace Approach to the "Global South": Insights from the Margins of a Popular Category. Third World Quarterly, 42(9), pp. 2018–2038.
Haug, S., Braveboy-Wagner, J., and Maihold, G. (2021). 'The "Global South" in the Study of World Politics: Examining a Meta Category. Third World Quarterly, 42(9), pp. 1923–1944.
Helleiner, E. (2014a). Forgotten Foundations of Bretton Woods: International Development and the Making of the Postwar Order. Cornell University Press.
Helleiner, E. (2014b). Southern Pioneers of International Development. Global Governance, 20(3), 375–388.
Hirschman, A. O. (1958). The Strategy of Economic Development. New Haven, CT: Yale University Press.
Hirschman, A. O. (1968). The Political Economy of Import-Substituting Industrialization in Latin America. The Quarterly Journal of Economics, 82(1), pp. 1–32.
Hirschman, A. O. (1971). A Bias for Hope: Essays on Development and Latin America. New Haven, CT: Yale University Press.
Hirschman, A. O. (1981). Essays in Trespassing: Economics to Politics and Beyond. Cambridge: Cambridge University Press.
Hirschman, A. O. (1982). 'The rise and decline of development economics', in Gersovitz, M., Diaz-Alejandro, C. F., Ranis, G., and Rosenzweig,M. (eds.) The Theory and Experience of Economic Development: Essays in Honor of Sir W. Arthur Lewis. London: George Allen and Unwin, pp. 372–390.
Hodgson, M. G. S. (1974/1975). The Venture of Islam: Conscience and History in a World Civilization (Vols. 1–3). Chicago: University of Chicago Press.
Hodgson, M. G. S. (1993). Rethinking World History: Essays on Europe, Islam, and World History. Cambridge: Cambridge University Press.
Hope, J., Freeman, C., Maclean, K., Pande, R. and Sou, G. (2022). Shifts to Global Development: Is This a Reframing of Power, Agency and Progress? Area, 54(2), pp. 154–158.

Horner, R. and Hulme, D. (2019a). From International to Global Development: New Geographies of 21st Century Development. Development and Change, 50(2), pp. 347–378.

Horner, R. and Hulme, D. (2019b). Global Development, Converging Divergence and Development Studies: A Rejoinder. Development and Change, 50(2), pp. 495–510.

Hountondji, P. (1996). African Philosophy: Myth and Reality. 2nd edn. Bloomington: Indiana University Press.

Hull, G. (2019). Contesting the Narrow Approach to Intellectual Decolonisation, or How Martin Heidegger Captured an African University. New Agenda: South African Journal of Social and Economic Policy, 2019(73), pp. 29–33.

Hull, G. (2021). Some Pitfalls of Decoloniality Theory. The Thinker, 89(4), pp. 63–74.

Hull, G. (2022). Epistemic Ethnonationalism: Identity Policing in Neo-Traditionalism and Decoloniality Theory. Acta Academica, 54(3), pp. 131–155.

Hulme, D. and Toye, J. (2006). The Case for Cross-Disciplinary Social Science Research on Poverty, Inequality and Well-Being. Journal of Development Studies, 42(7), 1085–1107.

Hulme, D. and Toye, J. (2007). 'The case for cross-disciplinary social science research on poverty, inequality and well-being', in Hulme, D. and Toye, J. (eds.) Understanding Poverty and Well-Being: Bridging the Disciplines. London: Routledge, pp. 1–23.

Ibn Khaldūn (1958). The Muqaddimah: An Introduction to History. Translated by F. Rosenthal. 3 vols. Princeton, NJ: Princeton University Press (Bollingen Series, reissued 1967).

Independent Commission on International Development Issues (1980). North–South: A Programme for Survival (The Brandt Report). London: Pan Books.

International Monetary Fund (2025). World Economic Outlook, April 2025: A Critical Juncture amid Policy Shifts. Washington, DC: IMF.

Ishmael, L. (2024). The New South: Breaking with the Past—West–South Engagement in a Changing World. IDOS Discussion Paper 9/2024. Bonn: German Institute of Development and Sustainability (IDOS).

Jackson, C. (2002). Disciplining Gender? World Development, 30(3), 497–509.

Jackson, T. (2009). Prosperity without Growth: Economics for a Finite Planet. London: Earthscan.

Johnson, P., and Papageorgiou, C. (2020). What Remains of Cross-Country Convergence? Journal of Economic Literature, 58(1), 129–175.

Kaldor, N. (1966). Causes of the Slow Rate of Economic Growth of the United Kingdom: An Inaugural Lecture. Cambridge: Cambridge University Press.

Kaldor, N. (1967). Strategic Factors in Economic Development. Ithaca, NY: New York State School of Industrial and Labor Relations, Cornell University.

Kanbur, R. (2002). Economics, Social Science and Development. World Development, 30(3), 477–486.

Kanbur, R. (2006). "What's Social Policy Got to Do With Economic Growth?", Cornell Dyson Working Paper. Also published in Indian Journal of Human Development 1(1), 3–19 (2007).

Kanbur, R. and Shaffer, P. (2007). Epistemology, Normative Theory and Poverty Analysis: Implications for Q-Squared in Practice. World Development, 35(2), 183–196.

Kanbur, R., Ortiz-Juarez, E., and Sumner, A. (2024). Is the Era of Declining Global Income Inequality Over? Structural Change and Economic Dynamics, 70, 45–55.

Kapoor, I. (2023). Decolonising Development Studies. Review of International Studies, 49(3), 346–355.

Kay, C. (1989). Latin American Theories of Development and Underdevelopment. London: Routledge.

Khokhar, T. and Serajuddin, U. (2015). Should We Continue to Use the Term "Developing World"? World Bank Open Data Blog. Available at: https://blogs.worldbank.org/en/opendata/should-we-continue-use-term-developing-world

Kiely, R. (1999). The Last Refuge of the Noble Savage? A Critical Assessment of Post-Development Theory. The European Journal of Development Research, 11(1), 30–55.

Klein, J. T. (2017). 'Typologies of interdisciplinarity: The boundary work of definition', in Frodeman,R. (ed.) The Oxford Handbook of Interdisciplinarity (2nd edn), 21–34. Oxford: Oxford University Press.
Kothari, A., Salleh, A., Escobar, A., Demaria, F., and Acosta, A. (eds.) (2019). Pluriverse: A Post-Development Dictionary. New Delhi: Tulika Books.
Kothari, U. (ed.) (2005a). A Radical History of Development Studies: Individuals, Institutions and Ideologies. London: Zed Books.
Kothari, U. (2005b). 'From colonial administration to development studies: A post-colonial critique of the history of development studies', in Kothari,U. (ed.) A Radical History of Development Studies: Individuals, Institutions and Ideologies, 47–66. London: Zed Books.
Kraay, A. (2006). When is Growth Pro-Poor? Evidence from a Panel of Countries. Journal of Development Economics, 80(1), 198–227.
Krishnan, A. (2009). What Are Academic Disciplines? Some Observations on the Disciplinarity vs. Interdisciplinarity Debate. NCRM Working Paper. Southampton: University of Southampton.
Kuhn, T. S. (1962). The Structure of Scientific Revolutions. Chicago: University of Chicago Press.
Lang, M. (2017). Degrowth – Unsuited for the Global South? Alternautas, 4(1), 100–113.
Lang, M. (2022). Buen Vivir as a Territorial Practice: Building a More Just and Sustainable Life through Interculturality. Sustainability Science, 17(4), 1287–1299.
Lang, M. and Mokrani, D. (eds) (2011). Más allá del desarrollo. Quito: Fundación Rosa Luxemburg/Abya-Yala. (Spanish original.) English translation: Lang, M. and Mokrani, D. (eds) (2013). Beyond Development: Alternative Visions from Latin America. Amsterdam/Quito: Transnational Institute and Rosa Luxemburg Stiftung.
Lasswell, H. D. (1936). Politics: Who Gets What, When, How. New York: McGraw-Hill.
Latouche, S. (2009). Farewell to Growth. Cambridge: Polity.
Lawson, T. (1997). Economics and Reality. London and New York: Routledge.
Lawson, T. (2003). Reorienting Economics. London and New York: Routledge.
Lawson, T. (2019). The Nature of Social Reality: Issues in Social Ontology. Abingdon and New York: Routledge.
Leach, M., MacGregor, H., Scoones, I., and Wilkinson, A. (2021). Post-Pandemic Transformations: How and Why COVID-19 Requires Us to Rethink Development. World Development, 138, 105233.
Leach, M., MacGregor, H., Scoones, I., and Taylor, P. (2024). Post-Pandemic Transformations and the Recasting of Development: A Comment and Further Reflections. Dev Change, 54(6): 1575–1593.
Lees, N. (2021). The Brandt Line after Forty Years: The More North–South Relations Change, the More They Stay the Same? Review of International Studies, 47(1), 85–106.
Lewis, D. (2019). "Big D" and "little d": Two Types of Twenty-First Century Development? Third World Quarterly, 40(11), pp. 1957–1975.
Lewis, W. A. (1944). An Economic Plan for Jamaica. Agenda, 3(4), November, pp. 154–163.
Lewis, W. A. (1949). Industrial Development in Puerto Rico. Caribbean Economic Review, 1(1–2), pp. 153–176.
Lewis, W. A. (1950). The Industrialisation of the British West Indies. Caribbean Economic Review, 2(1), May, pp. 1–61.
Lewis, W. A. (1953). Report on Industrialisation and the Gold Coast. Accra: Government Printing Department.
Lewis, W. A. (1954). Economic Development with Unlimited Supplies of Labour. The Manchester School, 22(2), pp. 139–191.
López-Calva, L. F. and Ortiz-Juárez, E. (2014). A Vulnerability Approach to the Definition of the Middle Class. The Journal of Economic Inequality, 12, pp. 23–47.
Loxley, J. (2004). What Is Distinctive about International Development Studies? Canadian Journal of Development Studies/Revue canadienne d'études du développement, 25(1), pp. 25–38.

Lugones, M. (2007). Heterosexualism and the Colonial/Modern Gender System. Hypatia, 22(1), pp. 186–209.
Lugones, M. (2010). Toward a Decolonial Feminism. Hypatia, 25(4), pp. 742–759.
MacGinty, R. and Williams, A. (2016). Conflict and Development. 2nd edn. London: Routledge.
Mahoney, J. (2010). Colonialism and Postcolonial Development: Spanish America in Comparative Perspective. Cambridge: Cambridge University Press.
Mahoney, J. and Thelen, K. (eds) (2009). Explaining Institutional Change: Ambiguity, Agency, and Power. Cambridge: Cambridge University Press.
Maldonado-Torres, N. (2011). Thinking through the Decolonial Turn: Post-Continental Interventions in Theory, Philosophy, and Critique—An Introduction. Transmodernity, 1(2), pp. 1–15.
Marchand, M. H. and Parpart, J. L. (eds.) (1995). Feminism/Postmodernism/ Development. London: Routledge.
Martinussen, J. (1997). Society, State and Market: A Guide to Competing Theories of Development. London: Zed Books.
Marx, K. (1867). Capital: A Critique of Political Economy. Volume I. Hamburg: Otto Meissner Verlag.
Matilal, B. K. (1981). The Central Philosophy of Jainism (Anekāntavāda). Ahmedabad: L. D. Institute of Indology.
Maxwell, S. (1998). Comparisons, Convergence and Connections: Development Studies in North and South. IDS Bulletin, 29(1), pp. 20–31.
Mayer, P. (1951). Two Studies in Applied Anthropology in Kenya. Colonial Research Studies Number 3. London: HMSO for the UK Colonial Office.
Mbiti, J. S. (1969). African Religions and Philosophy. London: Heinemann.
McGregor, J. A. (2007). 'Researching wellbeing: From concepts to methodology', in Gough, I. and McGregor, J. A. (eds.) Wellbeing in Developing Countries. Cambridge: Cambridge University Press, pp. 316–350.
Mehta, L., Haug, R., and Haddad, L. (2006). Reinventing Development Research. Forum for Development Studies, 33(1), pp. 143–148.
Melber, H., Kothari, U., Camfield, L., and Biekart, K. (eds) (2024). Challenging Global Development: Towards Decoloniality and Justice. Cham: Springer Nature.
Mignolo, W. D. (2002). The Geopolitics of Knowledge and the Colonial Difference. South Atlantic Quarterly, 101(1), pp. 57–96.
Mignolo, W. D. (2007). Delinking: The Rhetoric of Modernity, the Logic of Coloniality and the Grammar of De-Coloniality. Cultural Studies, 21(2–3), pp. 449–514.
Mignolo, W. D. (2009). Epistemic Disobedience, Independent Thought and De-Colonial Freedom. Theory, Culture and Society, 26(7–8), pp. 159–181.
Mignolo, W. D. (2011). The Darker Side of Western Modernity: Global Futures, Decolonial Options. Durham, NC: Duke University Press.
Mignolo, W. D. (2021). The Politics of Decolonial Investigations. Durham, NC: Duke University Press.
Mitra, S., Palmer, M., and Vuong, V. A. (2020). Development and Interdisciplinarity: A Citation Analysis. World Development, 135, 105076.
Mkandawire, T. (2001). Thinking about Developmental States in Africa. Cambridge Journal of Economics, 25(3), pp. 289–314.
Mkandawire, T. (2010). Aid, Accountability, and Democracy in Africa. Social Research, 77(4), 1149–1182.
Molteberg, E. and Bergstrøm, C. (2000). Our Common Discourse: Diversity and Paradigms in Development Studies (Paper No. 1 of 2). NORAGRIC Working Paper No. 20. Ås: Agricultural University of Norway, NORAGRIC.
Moosavi, L. (2020). The Decolonial Bandwagon and the Dangers of Intellectual Decolonisation. International Review of Sociology, 30(2), pp. 332–354.
Mouzelis, N. (1995). Sociological Theory: What Went Wrong? Diagnosis and Remedies. London: Routledge.

Munck, R. and O'Hearn, D. (eds) (1999). Critical Development Theory: Contributions to a New Paradigm. London: Zed Books.
Munro, L. T. (2023). Are the SDGs a Hegemonic Global Policy Agenda? Evidence from National Development Plans. Revue internationale des études du développement, 253, pp. 33–61.
Myrdal, G. (1957). Economic Theory and Under-Developed Regions. London: Gerald Duckworth.
Nabudere, D. W. (2005). Ubuntu Philosophy: Memory and Reconciliation. Kigali. Centre for Basic Research.
Narayan, D., Patel, R., Schafft, K., Rademacher, A., and Koch-Schulte, S. (2000a). Voices of the Poor: Can Anyone Hear Us? Washington, DC: World Bank.
Narayan, D., Chambers, R., Shah, M. K., and Petesch, P. (2000b). Voices of the Poor: Crying Out for Change. Washington, DC: World Bank.
Ndlovu-Gatsheni, S. J. (2013). Coloniality of Power in Postcolonial Africa: Myths of Decolonization. Dakar: CODESRIA.
Ndlovu-Gatsheni, S. J. (2018). Epistemic Freedom in Africa: Deprovincialization and Decolonization. London: Routledge.
Ndlovu-Gatsheni, S. J. (2020). Decolonization, Development and Knowledge in Africa: Turning over a New Leaf. London: Routledge.
Nkrumah, K. (1965). Neo-Colonialism: The Last Stage of Imperialism. London: Thomas Nelson and Sons.
North, D. C. (1990). Institutions, Institutional Change and Economic Performance. Cambridge: Cambridge University Press.
North, D. C. (1991). Institutions. Journal of Economic Perspectives, 5(1): 97–112.
North, D. C. (2005a). Understanding the Process of Economic Change. Princeton, NJ: Princeton University Press.
North, D. C. (2005b). 'Institutions and the performance of economies over time', in Ménard, C. and Shirley, M. M. (eds.) Handbook of New Institutional Economics. Boston: Springer, pp. 21–30.
Nussbaum, M. C. (2011). Creating Capabilities: The Human Development Approach. Cambridge, MA: Harvard University Press.
Nyerere, J. K. (1966). Freedom and Unity: Uhuru na umoja. A Selection from Writings and Speeches, 1952–1965. Dar es Salaam: Oxford University Press.
Nyerere, J. K. (1968). Freedom and Socialism: Uhuru na ujamaa. A Selection from Writings and Speeches, 1965–1967. Dar es Salaam: Oxford University Press.
OECD (2003). Harmonising Donor Practices for Effective Aid Delivery. Paris: OECD.
Oglesby, C. (1969). Vietnamism Has Failed... The Revolution can Only Be Mauled, Not Defeated. Commonweal, 90 (Special issue on Vietnam), 21 March 1969, pp. 11–12.
Okoth, K. O. (2023). Red Africa: Reclaiming Revolutionary Black Politics. London: Verso.
Oldekop, J. A., Horner, R., Hulme, D., Adhikari, R., Agarwal, B., Alford, M., Bakewell, O., Banks, N., Barrientos, S., Bastia, T., Bebbington, A., Das, U., Dimova, R., Duncombe, R., Enns, C., Fielding, D., Foster, C., Foster, T., Frederiksen, T., Gao, P., Gillespie, T., Heeks, R., Hickey, S., Hess, M., Jepson, N., Karamchedu, A., Kothari, U., Krishnan, A., Lavers, T., Mamman, A., Mitlin, D., Monazam Tabrizi, N., Müller, T. R., Nadvi, K., Pasquali, G., Pritchard, R., Pruce, K., Rees, C., Renken, J., Savoia, A., Schindler, S., Surmeier, A., Tampubolon, G., Tyce, M., Unnikrishnan, V., and Zhang, Y.-F. (2020). COVID-19 and the Case for Global Development. World Development, 134.
Onaran, Ö. (2019). 'Equality-led development and the demand- and supply-side effects', Development and Change, 50(2), 445–457.
Ordóñez Llanos, A., Taylor, P., Khanduja, G., Nelson, E., and Mamoun, T. (2024). Envisioning an Equitable Future for Research across the North–South Divide. Lima, Peru: Southern Voice.
Osterhammel, J. (2018). Unfabling the East: The Enlightenment's Encounter with Asia. Princeton, NJ: Princeton University Press.

Pahl, S. and Timmer, M. P. (2020). Do Global Value Chains Enhance Economic Upgrading? A Long View. Journal of Development Studies, 56(9), 1683–1705.
Pailey, R. N. (2020). De-centring the "White Gaze" of Development. Development and Change, 51(3), 729–745.
Palma, J. G. (2005). 'Four sources of "de-industrialization" and a new concept of the "Dutch disease"', in Ocampo, J. A. (ed.) Beyond Reforms: Structural Dynamics and Macroeconomic Vulnerability. Stanford, CA/Washington, DC: Stanford University Press and World Bank, pp. 71–116.
Palma, J. G. (2008). 'Deindustrialisation, premature deindustrialisation, and the Dutch disease', in Durlauf, S. N. and Blume, L. E. (eds.) The New Palgrave Dictionary of Economics (2nd ed.). Basingstoke: Palgrave Macmillan, pp. 401–410.
Palma, J. G. (2006). Globalizing Inequality: "Centrifugal" and "Centripetal" Forces at Work. UN DESA Working Paper No. 35, ST/ESA/2006/DWP/35. New York: United Nations.
Patel, D., Sandefur, J. and Subramanian, A. (2021). The New Era of Unconditional Convergence. Journal of Development Economics, 152, 102687.
Patel, K. (2020). Race and a Decolonial Turn in Development Studies. Third World Quarterly, 41(9), 1463–1475.
Pattanaik, B. K. (2016). Introduction to Development Studies. New Delhi: SAGE India.
Peacock, A. T. and Dosser, D. G. (1958). The National Income of Tanganyika, 1952–54. Colonial Research Studies No. 26. London: HMSO.
Peet, R. and Hartwick, E. (2015). Theories of Development: Contentions, Arguments, Alternatives (3rd ed.). New York/London: Guilford Press.
Phillips, N. (2017). Power and Inequality in the Global Political Economy. International Affairs, 93(2), pp. 429–444.
Popper, K. R. (1959). The Logic of Scientific Discovery. London: Hutchinson. Original German edition: Logik der Forschung. Vienna: Julius Springer, 1934.
Prebisch, R. (1950 [1949 Spanish]).The Economic Development of Latin America and Its Principal Problems. New York: United Nations.
QS (2025). QS World University Rankings by Subject 2025: Development Studies [online]. Available at: https://www.topuniversities.com/university-subject-rankings/development-studies (Accessed 15 September 2025).
Quijano, A. (2000). Coloniality of Power and Eurocentrism in Latin America. International Sociology, 15(2), pp. 215–232.
Quijano, A. (2007). Coloniality and Modernity/Rationality. Cultural Studies, 21(2–3), pp. 168–178.
Rahnema, M. (1997). 'Towards post-development: Searching for signposts, a new language and new paradigms', in Rahnema, M. and Bawtree, V. (eds) The Post-Development Reader. London: Zed Books, pp. 377–403.
Ramose, M. B. (1999). African Philosophy through Ubuntu. Harare: Mond Books.
Rist, G. (2008). The History of Development: From Western Origins to Global Faith. 3rd edn. London: Zed Books.
Rodney, W. (1972). How Europe Underdeveloped Africa. London: Bogle-L'Ouverture Publications.
Rodrik, D. (2013). Unconditional Convergence in Manufacturing. Quarterly Journal of Economics, 128(1), 165–204.
Rodrik, D. (2016). Premature Deindustrialization. Journal of Economic Growth, 21(1), pp. 1–33.
Room, G. (2000). Commodification and Decommodification: A Developmental Critique. Policy and Politics, 28(3), pp. 331–351.
Rosenstein-Rodan, P. N. (1943). Problems of Industrialisation of Eastern and South-Eastern Europe. The Economic Journal, 53(210/211), 202–211.
Rosenstein-Rodan, P. N. (1944). The international development of economically backward areas. International Affairs, 20(2), 157–165.
Rostow, W. W. (1960). The Stages of Economic Growth: A Non-Communist Manifesto. Cambridge: Cambridge University Press.

Rue, L. D. (1994). By the Grace of Guile: The Role of Deception in Natural History and Human Affairs. New York: Oxford University Press.
Rutazibwa, O. U. (2018). 'On babies and bathwater: decolonizing International Development Studies', in de Jong, S., Icaza, R., and Rutazibwa, O. U. (eds) Decolonization and Feminisms in Global Teaching and Learning. London: Routledge, pp. 158–180.
Sachs, W. (ed.) (1992). The Development Dictionary: A Guide to Knowledge as Power. London: Zed Books.
Said, E. W. (1978). Orientalism. New York: Pantheon Books.
Said, E. W. (1983). The World, the Text, and the Critic. Cambridge, MA: Harvard University Press.
Said, E. W. (1993). Culture and Imperialism. London: Chatto and Windus.
Saith, A. (2006). From Universal Values to Millennium Development Goals: Lost in Translation. Development and Change, 37(6), pp. 1167–1199.
Sauvy, A. (1952). Trois mondes, une planète. L'Observateur, 14 August.
Scheyvens, R. and Storey, D. (eds.) (2003). Development Fieldwork: A Practical Guide. London: SAGE.
Schumpeter, J. A. (1934). The Theory of Economic Development. Cambridge, MA: Harvard University Press.
Schuurman, F. J. (ed.) (1993). Beyond the Impasse: New Directions in Development Theory. London: Zed Books.
Searle, J. R. (2005). What Is an Institution? Journal of Institutional Economics, 1(1), pp. 1–22.
Seers, D. (1963). The Limitations of the Special Case. Bulletin of the Oxford University Institute of Economics and Statistics, 25(2), pp. 77–98.
Seers, D. (1969). The Meaning of Development. International Development Review, 11(4), pp. 3–4.
Seers, D. (1979). 'The periphery of Europe', in Seers, D., Schaffer, B., and Kiljunen, M.-L. (eds) Underdeveloped Europe: Studies in Core-Periphery Relations. Hassocks, Sussex: Harvester Press, pp. 3–34.
Seers, D., Schaffer, B., and Kiljunen, M. -L. (eds.) (1979). Underdeveloped Europe: Studies in Core-Periphery Relations. Hassocks, Sussex: Harvester Press. (Atlantic Highlands, NJ: Humanities Press US edn.)
Sen, A. (1985). Well-Being, Agency and Freedom: The Dewey Lectures 1984. The Journal of Philosophy, 82(4), 169–221.
Sen, A. K. (1999). Development as Freedom. New York: Alfred A. Knopf.
Senghor, L. S. (1964). On African Socialism. New York: Frederick A. Praeger.
Shaffer, P. (2023). Growth, Poverty and Immiserizing Growth: Empirical Evidence. Q-Squared Working Paper No. 72. Peterborough, ON: Trent University, Department of International Development Studies. Available at: https://www.trentu.ca/ids/sites/trentu.ca.ids/files/documents/Q2WP72_Shaffer%20(1).pdf
Shaffer, P. (2024). Immiserizing Growth Fails the Poor: Theory and Empirical Research. Oxford: Oxford University Press.
Shaffer, P., Kanbur, R., and Sandbrook, R. (eds.) (2019). Immiserizing Growth: When Growth Fails the Poor. Oxford: Oxford University Press.
Shiva, V. (1993). Monocultures of the Mind: Perspectives on Biodiversity and Biotechnology London: Zed Books.
Singer, H. W. (1950). The Distribution of Gains between Investing and Borrowing Countries. American Economic Review, 40(2), pp. 473–485.
Smith, L. T. (1999). Decolonizing Methodologies: Research and Indigenous Peoples. London and New York: Zed Books.
Smith, M. N. and Lester, C.-A. (2023). From "Dependency" to "Decoloniality"? The Enduring Relevance of Materialist Political Economy and the Problems of a "Decolonial" Alternative. Social Dynamics, 49(2), pp. 196–219.
Sondarjee, M. and Andrews, N. (2023). Decolonizing International Relations and Development Studies: What's in a Buzzword? International Journal, 77(4), pp. 551–571.

Spivak, G. C. (1988). 'Can the Subaltern Speak?', in Nelson, C. and Grossberg, L. (eds) Marxism and the Interpretation of Culture. Urbana and Chicago: University of Illinois Press, pp. 271–313.

Spivak, G. C. (1999). A Critique of Postcolonial Reason: Toward a History of the Vanishing Present. Cambridge, MA: Harvard University Press.

Statman, A. (2019). The First Global Turn: Chinese Contributions to Enlightenment World History. Journal of World History, 30(3), 363–392.

Statman, A. (2023). A Global Enlightenment: Western Progress and Chinese Science. Chicago: UCP.

Steinmetz, G. (ed.) (2005). The Politics of Method in the Human Sciences: Positivism and Its Epistemological Others. Durham, NC: Duke University Press.

Streeten, P. P. (1979). 'Basic Needs: Premises and Promises. Journal of Policy Modeling, 1(1), pp. 136–146.

Sud, N. and Sánchez-Ancochea, D. (2022). Southern Discomfort: Interrogating the Category of the Global South. Development and Change, 53(6), pp. 1123–1150.

Sumner, A. (2016). Global Poverty: Deprivation, Distribution, and Development since the Cold War. Oxford: Oxford University Press.

Sumner, A. (2021). Deindustrialization, Distribution, and Development: Structural Change in the Global South. Oxford University Press.

Sumner, A. and Tribe, M. A. (2008). International Development Studies: Theories and Methods in Research and Practice. London: Sage.

Sumner, A. and Yusuf, A. A. (2024a). 'The Shifting and Increased Complexity of Global Poverty And Inequalities', in OECD Development Co-operation Report 2024: Tackling Poverty and Inequalities through the Green Transition. Paris: OECD.

Sumner, A. and Yusuf, A. A. (2024b). New Estimates of the Cost of Ending Poverty and its Global Distribution. UNU-WIDER Working Paper 2024/46. Helsinki: UNU-WIDER.

Sumner, A., Ortiz-Juarez, E., and Hoy, C. (2022). Measuring Global Poverty before and during the Pandemic: A Political Economy of Overoptimism. Third World Quarterly, 43(1), pp. 1–17.

Sunkel, O. (1966). The Structural Background of Development Problems in Latin America', Weltwirtschaftliches Archiv, 97, pp. 22–63.

Szirmai, A. (2012). Industrialisation as an Engine of Growth in Developing Countries, 1950–2005. Structural Change and Economic Dynamics, 23(4), pp. 406–420.

Táíwò, O. (2022). Against Decolonisation: Taking African Agency Seriously. London: Hurst.

Taylor, P. and Tremblay, C. (2022). Decolonising Knowledge for Development in the Covid-19 Era. Brighton: Institute of Development Studies (IDS).

Taylor, P., Camfield, L., Abreu, A., Grabowski, M., Mishra, N., and Tremblay, C. (2024). Reflections on Decolonising Knowledge for Development: An Invitation to an EADI Conversation. EADI Reflection Paper, January 2024. Bonn: EADI.

Tilly, C. (1984). Big Structures, Large Processes, Huge Comparisons. New York, NY: Russell Sage Foundation.

Timmer, M. P., Erumban, A. A., Los, B., Stehrer, R. and De Vries, G. J. (2014). Slicing up Global Value Chains. Journal of Economic Perspectives, 28(2), pp. 99–118.

Toye, J. (1987). Dilemmas of Development: Reflections on the Counter-Revolution in Development Theory and Policy. Oxford: Basil Blackwell.

Tribe, M. (2009). A Short History of the Development Studies Association. Journal of International Development, vol. 21(6), pp. 732–741.

Truman, H. S. (1949). Inaugural Address, 20 January 1949.

Turner, S. (2000). 'What are disciplines? And how is interdisciplinarity different?', in Weingart, P. and Stehr, N. (eds) Practising Interdisciplinarity. Toronto: University of Toronto Press, pp. 46–65.

Wade, R. (1990). Governing the Market: Economic Theory and the Role of Government in East Asian Industrialization. Princeton, NJ: Princeton University Press.

Wade, R. H. (2018). The Developmental State: Dead or Alive? Development and Change, 49(2), pp. 518–546.
Wallerstein, I. (1974a). The Modern World-System I: Capitalist Agriculture and the Origins of the European World-Economy in the Sixteenth Century. New York: Academic Press.
Wallerstein, I. (1974b). The Rise and Future Demise of the World Capitalist System. Comparative Studies in Society and History, 16(4): 387–415.
Wallerstein, I. (1976). Semi-Peripheral Countries and the Contemporary World Crisis. Theory and Society, 3(4), pp. 461–483.
Wallerstein, I. (1980). The Modern World-System II: Mercantilism and the Consolidation of the European World-Economy, 1600–1750. New York: Academic Press.
Wallerstein, I. (1989). The Modern World-System III: The Second Era of Great Expansion of the Capitalist World-Economy, 1730s–1840s. San Diego, CA: Academic Press.
Wallerstein, I. (1997). Eurocentrism and Its Avatars: The Dilemmas of Social Science. Sociological Bulletin, 46(1), pp. 21–39.
Wallerstein, I. (2011). The Modern World-System IV: Centrist Liberalism Triumphant, 1789–1914. Berkeley, CA: University of California Press.
Wheeler, D. (2011). Quantifying Vulnerability to Climate Change: Implications for Adaptation Assistance. CGD Working Paper No. 240. Washington, DC: Center for Global Development.
Wiebe, K., Robinson, S., and Cattaneo, A. (2019). 'Climate change, agriculture and food security: Impacts and the potential for adaptation and mitigation', in Campanhola, C. and Pandey, S. (eds.) Sustainable Food and Agriculture: An Integrated Approach. Amsterdam: Elsevier/FAO, pp. 55–74.
Wiegratz, J., Behuria, P., Laskaridis, C., Pheko, L. L., Radley, B., and Stevano, S. (2023). Common Challenges for All? A Critical Engagement with the Emerging Vision for Post-pandemic Development Studies. Development and Change, 54(5), pp. 921–953.
Willis, K. (2005). Theories and Practices of Development. London: Routledge.
Wilson, K. (2012). Race, Racism and Development: Interrogating History, Discourse and Practice. London: Zed Books.
Wiredu, K. (1996). Cultural Universals and Particulars: An African Perspective. Bloomington, IN: Indiana University Press.
Wiredu, K. (1980). Philosophy and an African Culture. Cambridge: Cambridge University Press.
Wood, G. (2003). Staying Secure, Staying Poor: The "Faustian Bargain". World Development, 31(3), pp. 455–471.
World Bank (2005). Poverty and Inequality Platform Database (downloaded at pip.worldbank.org).
World Bank (2020). World Development Report 2020: Trading for Development in the Age of Global Value Chains. Washington, DC: World Bank.
World Bank (2023). Macro Poverty Outlook for Latin America and the Caribbean, April 2023. Washington, DC: World Bank.
World Bank (2024). World Development Indicators [online database]. Washington, DC: World Bank. Available at: https://databank.worldbank.org/source/world-development-indicators
World Bank. (2025). World Development Indicators. Washington, DC: World Bank.
Ziai, A. (2019). Towards a More Critical Theory of "Development" in the 21st Century. Development and Change, 50(2), pp. 458–467.

Index

For the benefit of digital users, indexed terms that span two pages (e.g., 52–53) may, on occasion, appear on only one of those pages.

Tables and figures are indicated by an italic *t* and *f*, following the paragraph number.

Please note that 'GN' stands for 'Global North', while 'GS' represents 'Global South', whenever appearing.